D0768403

WHAT
YOU
TAKE
WITH
YOU

WHAT YOU TAKE WITH YOU

THERESE GREENWOOD

UNIVERSITY *of* ALBERTA PRESS

Wildfire, Family and the Road Home

Published by

The University of Alberta Press
Ring House 2
Edmonton, Alberta, Canada T6G 2E1
www.uap.ualberta.ca

Copyright © 2019 Therese Greenwood

LIBRARY AND ARCHIVES CANADA
CATALOGUING IN PUBLICATION

Title: What you take with you : wildfire, family
 and the road home / Therese Greenwood.
Names: Greenwood, Therese, author.
Series: Wayfarer (Edmonton, Alta.)
Description: Series statement: Wayfarer
 series
Identifiers: Canadiana (print) 20190056541 |
 Canadiana (ebook) 20190056592 |
 ISBN 9781772124491 (softcover) |
 ISBN 9781772124712 (PDF) |
 ISBN 9781772124699 (EPUB) |
 ISBN 9781772124705 (Kindle)
Subjects: LCSH: Greenwood, Therese. |
 LCSH: Wildfires—Alberta—Fort
 McMurray—History—21st century. |
 LCSH: Wildfires—Alberta—Fort
 McMurray—Anecdotes. | LCSH: Disaster
 victims—Alberta—Fort McMurray—
 Biography. | LCSH: Disaster relief—
 Alberta—Fort McMurray—Anecdotes.
Classification: LCC SD421.34.C2 G74 2019 |
 DDC 363.37/8092—dc23

First edition, first printing, 2019.
First printed and bound in Canada by
Houghton Boston Printers, Saskatoon,
Saskatchewan.
Copyediting by Kimmy Beach.
Proofreading by Maya Fowler Sutherland.

All rights reserved. No part of this publication
may be reproduced, stored in a retrieval
system, or transmitted in any form or by any
means (electronic, mechanical, photocopying,
recording, or otherwise) without prior written
consent. Contact University of Alberta Press
for further details.

University of Alberta Press supports
copyright. Copyright fuels creativity,
encourages diverse voices, promotes free
speech, and creates a vibrant culture. Thank
you for buying an authorized edition of this
book and for complying with the copyright
laws by not reproducing, scanning, or
distributing any part of it in any form without
permission. You are supporting writers
and allowing University of Alberta Press to
continue to publish books for every reader.

University of Alberta Press is committed to
protecting our natural environment. As part
of our efforts, this book is printed on Enviro
Paper: it contains 100% post-consumer
recycled fibres and is acid- and chlorine-free.

University of Alberta Press gratefully
acknowledges the support received for its
publishing program from the Government
of Canada, the Canada Council for the Arts,
and the Government of Alberta through the
Alberta Media Fund.

Canada

Canada Council Conseil des Arts
for the Arts du Canada

Alberta
Government

In What You Take With You, *Therese Greenwood tells a very personal story of the Fort McMurray Wildfire. By considering the things that she lost in the blaze and the things that were saved, Greenwood takes the reader with her through her own evacuation, the road to safety, the grief that she experienced on losing her home, and the steps to her recovery. It is a beautiful book, sharply observed in the accounting of a disaster that affected the nation, gripping in the particulars of her own journey, and expansive in the questions it poses for us all: How is memory tied to the things we've collected, and what does it mean to make a home?*

—MIRANDA HILL, *author of* Sleeping Funny

Therese Greenwood's gripping account of the Fort McMurray wildfire evacuation, the largest and most devastating in Canadian history, is told in the deceptively relaxed manner that often masks true tragedy. You'll read this book with a mounting sense of panic. You'll look around your own house, imagining flames licking at your doors. You have two minutes: what would you save?

—WAYNE GRADY, *author of* Up From Freedom

My eyes filled with tears more than once while reading this book. So terrifying and so tender, it looks clearly and deeply into how we can survive loss and how our treasured objects can be the priceless vessels that carry the stories of both our past and our future.

—DIANE SCHOEMPERLEN, *author of* This Is Not My Life: A Memoir of Love, Prison, and Other Complications

For Steve

They whom we love and lose are no longer where they were before.
They are now wherever we are.
—SAINT JOHN CHRYSOSTOM

I don't mind a reasonable amount of trouble.
—DASHIELL HAMMETT

CONTENTS

PROLOGUE

MY SISTERS AND I grew up afraid we would die in a fire. There were a few reasons we thought our home would burn down and kill us. A few times it almost happened—the four of us running out into the night in our pajamas, feet crammed into the bedroom slippers we kept lined up on the floor next to us as we slept, tying up the belts to the robes that we hung on our bedposts every night, seeking the shelter of a car.

Much later, an adult living a well-ordered life in a prosperous city in northern Alberta, I no longer kept my slippers where I could find them in the dark. I was a wife, a homeowner, a public servant with a decent history of emergency management training. I thought I had put those childhood days behind me: running through smoke with a pounding heart was over and done with. I didn't even dream about it anymore. I never shared those memories, except with my sisters. Sometimes we would recall random details: a broken pair of glasses, a man's checked flat cap, an album of Christmas music, an old-fashioned crokinole board game, something long in the past. I never thought of writing about it. There was no point stirring up those ashes.

I can't believe I thought those ashes had been smothered, that the embers of my past weren't smouldering beneath the undergrowth, ready to burst into flames with the right fuel.

Of course, it was a fire that reignited it. There I was, decades after the first time a fire forced me to run from my home, once again sitting in a car and watching flames move towards the things I loved and towards me. This time, though, it wasn't a domestic tragedy. This time I was fleeing the Fort McMurray wildfire, a fire so great it had its own name: The Beast. I was in the middle of one of the biggest evacuations in the history of the country, hundreds of kilometres from the nearest city and escaping on the only highway out of town.

And I found myself carrying pieces of a past I thought I had let go. That is, until those pieces turned out to be the only things I reached for on my way out the door.

As I ran from my home for the last time, about to spend most of the next fifteen hours inching my way along roads crowded with other families seeking sanctuary, I was travelling in a car I had packed full of ghosts.

1 | BEFORE

"I LOOK AROUND MY HOME," people say to me, "and I imagine what I would take if there was a fire."

I heard that a lot after the wildfire in Fort McMurray, when Canadians watched shocking media images of an out-of-control inferno bearing down on a community—my community—and eighty thousand souls on the one road to safety.

Everyone tells me what they would pack if they were caught in a similar situation—usually baby and wedding photos, something sentimental. The younger ones mention laptop computers, hard drives, phones. "My phone is my life," they say.

What you think you will pack as you look around your comfortable living room and what you snatch when smoke chokes the air and flames lick the sky are entirely different. The people of Fort McMurray, who bundled their families into oversized pickups and late-model sedans and headed out on the highway towing all-terrain vehicles, boats and campers, tended to treat the random items they grabbed as a joke.

This is typical of the local sense of humour—a fierce, proud, self-deprecating wit borrowed from the east coast of Canada, Fort

McMurray being "the second-largest city in Newfoundland," as the saying goes. Every third person seems to come from "The Rock," part of the economic diaspora that, with the downturn in oil prices in the two years before the fire, had started flowing in the opposite direction.

The day after the evacuation I sat in an Edmonton hotel room and scrolled through social media posts about the seemingly zany items people snatched up as they fled their homes. Mismatched shoes. Individually-wrapped cheese slices. A Ziploc bag of smelts. A stuffed bear head. A Mason jar of home-canned moose meat. Each post included a comment along the lines of, "I hope this is one delicious pineapple!"

I had my lucky pen in my hand when my husband, Steve, called from his office to tell me about the evacuation order and the rapidly approaching fire. It's a thin, chrome-plated pen, but I have small hands and I like the way it feels. I imagine myself autographing books with it. When I dumped my purse on the hotel bed the next day, there it was. I texted a photo to a friend and said, "Good thing I saved my lucky pen. I have a lot of forms to fill out."

The complete evacuation of Fort McMurray happened on the first Tuesday of the month: May third, 2016. That meant Steve and I had changed up our morning routine. For months, we had carpooled to work, listening to public radio and drinking good coffee from environmentally friendly travel mugs, slipping into another day in our easy, well-ordered lives. We ate healthy meals and watched old movies on a specialty cable channel. My husband cycled and followed the Tour de France. I belonged to a national mystery writers' association and chatted about books on social media. We went to the public library once a month. We walked McMurray's boreal forest trails in good weather and exercised on our treadmill during cold winter months. We moved effortlessly with the rhythms of the town we had moved to four years before.

The first Tuesday of the month was discount day at a local supermarket with a good selection of organic produce. To get ahead of the

rush—which starts around noon in McMurray after shifts change and kids are delivered to school and daycare—I dropped Steve at his job and drove the few blocks along Franklin Avenue, the main downtown street, and spent the next hour buying two hundred and fifty dollars' worth of groceries.

I didn't need to stop for gas. Steve had intended to wash the car the night before. The car wash was closed but he gassed up anyway, so the trip wasn't a total waste. Buying that gas turned out to be the best decision Steve made that week.

That Tuesday was a beautiful morning, one of the nicest spring days I had seen during my four years in what I learned to call "McMurray." Dropping the "Fort" from the name marked me as a local and not one of the fly-in-fly-out workers who skip past the town to stay in camps on industry sites and then take their wages back to communities from one coast of Canada to the other. I also learned to avoid the diminutive "Fort Mac," which locals link to negative boom-town stereotypes, and to never, ever, call it "Fort McMoney."

Our first year in McMurray there had been snow on the ground in early May but that day the temperature was headed towards a record high, the heat usually expected in July and August. I wore my bright red rubber boots on most spring days, the better to track mud, but now I wore flip-flops I had hastily pulled from the bottom of a stack of as-yet-unpacked summer clothes in the back of our basement closest.

We lived on a short and pretty street in Riverview Heights, a small subdivision built a decade earlier in the north end of the Abasand neighbourhood. The brick house we had left in downtown Kingston, Ontario, was built by a Great Lakes shipwright in the early 1890s, with lathe and plaster and uneven floor boards, like most houses in the core of that three-hundred-year-old city. Everything about McMurray looked brand new.

We liked the Abasand neighbourhood the moment we saw it, built on top of a hill that rises above the length of McMurray's downtown core like a ship at dock. The bow of that ship, where our house was,

juts out over the Athabasca River. The western side, away from downtown, is carved by the Horse River flowing north to the Athabasca, and the whole neighbourhood was surrounded by a walking trail that provided views of the seemingly endless boreal forest. The houses were well-kept, most owner-occupied, sometimes with three generations under one roof. We joked that it looked like the neighbourhood the earnest George Bailey wanted to build in the Frank Capra movie *It's a Wonderful Life*.

I always pictured our neighbourhood when I read stories about the community. As the centre of Canada's oil sands industry, Fort McMurray is frequently profiled by national and international mainstream media, on social media and in old-fashioned word-of-mouth gossip. Before the wildfire, the town was inevitably described as post-apocalyptic-*Road-Warrior*-meets-Yukon-gold-rush. Instead of biker gangs and prostitutes and khat smokers, we saw swing sets, tricycles and kids jumping up and down in their yards when the ice cream truck drove by playing "When the Saints Go Marching In." You could tell the seasons by the large inflatable Santa Clauses and Easter bunnies and jack-o'-lanterns decorating the front yards. A few months before, the neighbourhood had been ablaze with Christmas decorations. With the sun setting around 3:00 PM on December twenty-first, the shortest day of the year, the town was determined, as one display said, to "rage against the dying of the light." I was skeptical the display organizers read the full poem but I appreciated the sentiment.

There was lots of sunlight by May, only six weeks before the summer solstice. Like many in the community, we were still figuratively blinking as we came out of winter hibernation, a communal cocooning prompted by average winter temperatures of minus twenty-seven degrees Celsius. The week of unexpectedly warm weather saw our neighbours putting up hanging flower baskets, sowing grass seed and digging in bedding for plants that liked short growing seasons and long days of sunlight. Even Steve and I had our small lawn aerated by a

local company that, two years before, would have been too busy for such a small job.

It was a sign of change that we could get this type of yard work done. Two years before, McMurray was booming so hard that City building inspectors couldn't keep up with permit applications. Now the contractors were actively competing for work that just months before would not have been worth their time. It was not as dire as some news reports had painted it, as oil companies continued to pump out the same number of barrels of oil each day, so workers related to production were still on the job. Those who worked on capital expansion projects and other supporting industries were not so fortunate. There had been a steady stream of layoffs as the oil downturn bit into the local economy, and three weeks before the fire I was laid off from my job, my position at the local college eliminated without warning.

After thirty years of continuous employment, I was adjusting from working twelve and sixteen hours a day to having to be nowhere in particular. I was not in a hurry as I drove home that day, making an effort to appreciate the sunny weather and turning on the air conditioning for the short drive because it was already thirty degrees Celsius. There was a smell of smoke in the air, but I wasn't concerned. My first summer in the north I was disconcerted by the wood smoke wafting in from forest fires sometimes as far away as the Yukon. But I adjusted, like everyone in town, and I was not unsettled by the nearby fire activity that had marked the weekend. The wind was blowing away from town, the smoke heading east, and the evacuation order issued over the weekend for a nearby McMurray neighbourhood had been lifted.

I backed into the garage so I could unload the groceries directly into the kitchen, a move that saved me precious seconds later on. I padded around our home for three-quarters of an hour stowing provisions in the basement freezer and in the kitchen pantry. I decided to delay my lunch and went to my upstairs office to work on the detective

novel I was writing now that I had time. I kept my office window open as I booted up the computer and listened to the little boys next door play a counting game. The older one had learned to count to twenty, while his younger brother could only make it to ten—he was clearly using his fingers. Count to twenty and hide and seek. Count to twenty and throw the ball. Count to twenty and run from one end of the yard to the other. The pair had so many toys outside—a trampoline, a motorized trike, a tent, bats, balls—when we moved in I mistook their home for a family-run day care.

Their parents were, like everyone else on our street, from Newfoundland. Steve and I were the only "Upper Canadians" and, in our early fifties, also the oldest people on the block. The average age of a McMurray resident is thirty-two and if I wanted to find Steve in the grocery store I looked for the only man with grey hair. With his high-top red sneakers, black jeans and sports jacket he stood out amid the pregnant women wearing yoga pants and pushing baby strollers and the young men in backward ball caps, work boots and reflective orange vests. Back in Kingston, full of retirees and academics, I frequently lost him in the crowd.

We also stood out in that we were the only people on the street who parked in our garage. Most of our neighbours had some version of the infamous McMurray "man cave": a garage filled with leather couches, large-screen televisions, tiki bars and billiard tables. Others stored boats, snowmobiles and ATVs, or used the space for elaborate woodworking projects and even to skin deer, hunting being a popular pastime. With no one parking in their garage, there was seldom a spare parking spot on our street.

We were also the only home with a single car, which we shared. We were proud of that, that we could manage with one vehicle, a fuel-efficient blue 2002 Honda CRV, which my nephew, who had lived with us one summer while he worked at a high-paying labourer job, called a "dad car." We had toyed with the idea of something newer, flashier, and sometimes we heard the siren call of satellite radio, Bluetooth and

USB outlets. We still had a cassette deck. But, most importantly, it was fuel-efficient.

There had been warning signs for a few days. The Sunday afternoon before the fire—the first day of May—Steve and I lounged in a living room recently filled with antique furniture inherited from my late father-in-law. We talked about starting a jigsaw puzzle on the extra-large pine coffee table and lazily discussed setting out the large wooden "Muskoka" lawn chairs on our front veranda. Then I heard the constant buzz of helicopters flying over our house. It wasn't unusual. We were on a flight path between the oil sands operations north of the city and the airport to the south. But this sounded like a busier back and forth than normal.

"Is there a fire?" I asked Steve.

I asked him because he was the web master for the municipality and he posted information at all hours. It turned out that there was a small forest fire on the northern edge of town, across the Athabasca and farther up Highway 63, the only paved route in and out of McMurray and the road that links neighbourhoods like ours and Beacon Hill and Gregoire south of the river to the neighbourhoods of Thickwood and Timberlea to the north. Helicopters were dipping down to the river, scooping up large buckets of water to douse the flames, circling over our home on their flight path.

"Why are you here?" I asked Steve a few times. For a time, I oversaw emergency public information for the region and I would have called my web guy to the Regional Emergency Operations Centre, the city's official mission control for emergency response located on the south end of town. But he checked and he wasn't called in.

"I can post any information from here," he said. And it wasn't any of my business but Steve didn't say that. I droned on about what I would do for emergency public information until Steve asked me if I wanted to go for a walk.

A walk was a good idea. It was too early in the year for mosquitoes and Steve assured me there were no bears. A provincial bear-catching

truck, which looks like a giant tin can on the back of a large pickup, was parked frequently near our street. The year before, someone in the neighbourhood had shot a bear that climbed one of his backyard trees. There had been no bears reported that weekend, so I scrambled in the closet for my red rubber boots.

"Don't bother with the boots," Steve said. "It's pretty dry."

I was skeptical. That was what he had said the year before when I ruined a good pair of running shoes, caking them with two inches of mud that never completely washed out. I shoved my feet into my new trail shoes, vowing as I laced them up that I would turn back if it was muddy. Steve was right. Our feet kicked up patches of dust as we walked, the trail as dry as if it had endured the summer's eighteen-hour sun even though it had been only two weeks since snow was on the ground.

We walked past the two houses to the end of our short street and onto the trail, a two-metre-wide path that the municipality tried to groom. It was supposedly closed to motorized traffic, but we were forced to step aside to allow several all-terrain vehicles to pass. The municipality had buried black plastic matting as a barrier for weeds along the trail, grooming the path with woodchips and mulch and placing concrete barriers at the entrances to make it pedestrians-only. But there was always someone who would hitch chains to a pickup truck and pull back the concrete barriers so he and his buddies could storm the walking path with ATVs. They rutted the trail with deep tire tracks, leaving the matting shredded, as they made their way into the boreal forest.

A report by the Royal Canadian Mounted Police, released a month after the fire, ruled out the possibility that lightning sparked the inferno—an obvious finding since there were no lightning strikes that day. The wildfire that came for us, the Mounties determined, started with "human activity." That is a needlessly polite way of saying a care-less idiot drove an ATV deep into the Crown Land along the Horse River on the western edge of Fort McMurray. Thousands of lives were

forever changed by that person, who drove one of the dozens of ATVs we heard roar past our home that weekend. All it took was one small decision to ignore municipally-ordered burn bans and fire department warnings about fire risks. One poorly extinguished campfire. One cigarette carelessly flicked aside. One stray spark from a hot exhaust pipe. Despite a public appeal by the Mounties for information, no one has ever come forward and admitted to being on the trail where the fire started.

I didn't spend much time fuming about ATVs that day. Steve and I walked the length of the western edge of our neighbourhood and talked of plans for our lawn, whether the tree we planted would grow and, if it didn't, it was okay because I had saved the receipt. We talked about when I would be able to sit outside to do my *New York Times* crossword puzzle. Would the white-throated sparrow with its "Poor Sam Peabody" cry—and the only songbird we recognized this far north—show up again to nest in the woods at the end of our road?

We also talked about something troubling me: a local media story about my layoff. A rookie reporter rushed to print without contacting me, his story posted online while I was still at work and sharing cake with colleagues, some of whom also received layoff notices. My employer, the local college, declined comment and avoided mentioning the others being laid off. The sole focus of the story was me, probably prompting the people of McMurray to ask, "Who the hell is Therese Greenwood and why do we care?" But getting laid off is tough, even in a town accustomed to it, and I was stung and embarrassed by the public nature of my departure.

I had a lot on my mind when we came to a lookout point by the Horse River, where we stopped to watch the helicopters swoop down, like hummingbirds at a feeder, to fill the water baskets. That was when we saw a new plume of smoke rising to the southwest, in the opposite direction of the fire being waterbombed by the helicopters. This plume rose straight into the bright blue sky in a tightly-wound column, the same slate grey as the tornado that spirits Dorothy away

from Kansas. It was too far away to hear the roar of the flames but the view was dramatic. From where we stood it was difficult to judge the distance. It looked close, only a few kilometres from our home.

"I need to get my camera," Steve said. He started his working career as a photojournalist and cannot resist a startling image. We hoofed it home and, it seems odd to say now, hurried back in the car in case the fire was over before we returned. We parked near the lookout and hopped over a small rail fence, awkwardly for me because I was carrying the camera's tripod, which two days later I would leave on the floor of the garage. As Steve set up his camera we were joined by other people, couples and dog walkers and a mountain biker, drawn by the smoke. We clustered a little too near the drop off to the Horse River.

"You better check your phone," I said to Steve. "They'll be calling you into the Emergency Operations Centre now."

No call came, so we moved further along the path, helicopters humming overhead as Steve looked for a different angle. When I look at his photographs now I see it was nearing the golden hour, that time precious to photographers when the sun starts to set and daylight is redder and softer. The setting sun glints off the plume of smoke and tints it pink-gold as it rises from the hill. The usually swampy green grass and bush cascading down the far hill look brown and dry, stark and cinematic, the landscape vast.

Steve was starting to pack up his camera, eager to get back to his computer and start photo editing, when I stopped him. "Take a head-shot of me," I said, and he laughed because headshots are one of our jokes. In the quarter of a century we've been together, Steve has taken dozens of my headshots, for columns when I was in the newspaper business, for announcements of new jobs, for speaking engagements at conferences and for short stories in mystery magazines. A few weeks before, snow still on the ground, he snapped a headshot for my social media feeds at almost the same spot on the trail. I was bundled up with a brand new red and purple scarf that had been a Christmas gift and a favourite light blue Columbia jacket I could not bear to

part with. It was golden hour then, too, the light burnished as the sun began to set. I felt like I was glowing. I look happy and confident, my grin easy as I look at Steve.

I was not feeling so photogenic as the smoke rose over my shoulder but I thought it would be a fun picture to send to my sisters in Ontario, in a look-how-close-I-am way. There is no winter coat this time. My arms are bare in a faded black T-shirt with a sagging collar, my face sweaty from stumbling around with the tripod, my eyes hidden by sunglasses. My right shoulder droops below my left and I am smirking because Steve is talking about the drop off behind me and cracking wise about a murder mystery writer found at the bottom of a cliff. Mostly, though, I look tired. After he took the shot, we headed home where I packed my emergency Go Bag.

Later that Sunday night, with the fire to the north barely under control, the fire to the southwest—soon to be named The Horse River Fire—officially became a big deal. The municipality first suggested a voluntary evacuation for residents of the Gregoire neighbourhood and a trailer park two kilometres south of Abasand, then changed it to a mandatory evacuation, declaring a localized state of emergency.

On Monday, conditions seemed back to normal. We awoke to learn that residents of Gregoire were allowed to return to their homes while provincial firefighting crews worked to contain a blaze that seemed to be moving further south. Only the trailer park on the outskirts of McMurray still faced an evacuation order. By the end of the day, the fire to the north was deemed extinguished, and the biggest concern seemed to be air quality for those downwind of The Horse River Fire.

Tuesday, May third, dawned radiant and sunny. The smoke that had filled the sky for nearly two days seemed to have disappeared, and the sky was a crisp, bright blue. What we didn't know was that something called a thermal inversion layer was simply holding the smoke close to the ground.

My Go Bag sat by my desk and I planned to unpack it as soon as I finished the daily word count I had set for myself. Around noon, I had

started the first lines of Chapter Four when my phone rang. It was Steve, who is an old-school type of employee who does not usually call home from work.

"Look out the window," he said.

I leaned back in my chair and poked my finger through the heavy wooden blinds. The sun was gone. Thick black smoke blanketed a sky that was bright blue thirty minutes before. The wind had shifted towards town.

2 | THE GO BAG

WHAT I DIDN'T KNOW, because the treetops of the boreal forest started forty metres from our home and blocked my view into the Horse River valley, was that I was looking at it from a different angle. Steve was on the second-highest floor of the city's tallest building, directly across from our home on the other side of the highway. He saw flames approaching Abasand, the narrow banks of the Horse River providing the only firebreak between our neighbourhood and the now raging wildfire. But he was calm and he knew that the Emergency Operations Centre had not ordered a mandatory evacuation.

"There's a voluntary evacuation notice for our neighbourhood," he said. "Come and get me so we can pack up."

"If I drive downtown to get you, we won't be able to get back in," I said. I knew that once I left the evacuation area, the police at the barricades would not allow me to re-enter the danger zone. "I'll pack up and come get you."

I hung up the phone and reached for the Go Bag sitting on the floor of my office. I'd packed Go Bags before. I had more than a decade of experience leading communications for municipal emergency

management teams. Most had a rule that anyone in the "Municipal Control Group," the body that takes over a city during an officially declared state of emergency, is subject to surprise inspections requiring you to produce your always-packed Go Bag. With communications staff on the lowest rung of every emergency team's pecking order, it was common knowledge I would be first on the snap inspection list. Waking up the fire chief or police chief in the middle of the night or interrupting the Mayor's Sunday barbecue was much less likely.

I loved being part of an emergency team and I liked having a Go Bag. It meant I was indispensable. I couldn't be expected to run out for toothpaste or a phone charger during an emergency. Accurate and timely public information can mean the difference between life and death—especially in a mass exodus of eighty thousand frightened people hoping they are not driving their families into a wall of flame.

It was important work but I also loved being part of something exciting. During the 2013 Alberta flood, better known for its impact on Calgary but also felt in McMurray, one of the young people with whom I worked pointed out that the colour-coded fluorescent vests we wore in the "war room"—mine was emblazoned with the initials "PIO" for Public Information Officer—were like the house sigils worn by medieval knights to denote their allegiance as they went into battle.

I enjoyed my work during the flood, particularly because no one was injured and the property damage relatively small. I was proud of getting a speeding ticket racing from the Emergency Ops Centre to City Hall for a press conference. I even liked the fact that I was running a fever of 102 and had a blistering cough but had to be on the job. I felt capable, well-trained, ready for anything.

Like the proverbial fire horse, even though I was no longer on an emergency team, I packed a Go Bag two days before the evacuation. Later, when we were safe in an Edmonton hotel, I wondered why I hadn't packed it in one of the nice leather bags in my closet. I had used the first bag I saw, a small green polyester knapsack with a rip along the zippered top. I packed as if I would be in a dedicated space at the

Emergency Operation Centre, not the boisterous madness of an emergency shelter, although the prescribed list of items is similar for both. The conventional wisdom is to pack for seventy-two hours and include passports and photo identification. Medication for seventy-two hours. A change of underwear for me (but not for Steve, I forgot that). Hand sanitizer. About one hundred and twenty dollars in cash. A backup memory stick of data and financial files. An extra set of house keys. In case of a power outage or downed cell towers, I had a pre-printed list of phone numbers and account numbers for everything from cable to phone to home security. I also set out a separate cloth bag printed with the slogan "Treat Me Like A Queen" to hold property deeds and insurance policies.

I stopped there deciding that, if we evacuated, I would fill a portable cooler with an ice pack and food and water from the refrigerator. This was stupid and I knew better but I didn't want Steve to think that the job loss had unsettled me and I was over-reacting. I should have packed granola bars, fruit and foodstuffs that did not need to be kept cold, as well as enough bottled water for seventy-two hours. Instead, when the evacuation happened, I opened the refrigerator I had just filled with groceries and hastily snatched all the food we would have for the next fifteen hours: Two cans of club soda. A cherry cola. A green apple. A single serving slice of cheese. Three pieces of red licorice. A single serving yogurt with no spoon.

After Steve's call, I jogged down the hallway from my home office into our bedroom to change from shorts and flip-flops into jeans and sneakers. I didn't want to trip as I ran up and down the stairs and I had seen the inside of evacuation shelters so I wanted to wear long pants, even though it was sweltering. Then I stuffed my phone in my pocket, accidentally pocket-dialed a friend, hefted the Go Bag and the Treat Me Like A Queen cloth bag of important files and ran down the stairs.

3 | THE ROLLING PIN

I ROUNDED THE CORNER at the bottom of the stairs and raced into the kitchen, skidding to a stop by the back door. I reached for the small-lidded porcelain bowl we kept on a shiny white stand to hold our keys. I picked up the bowl and carried it outside, fishing out the keys as I walked into an upside-down world.

The morning's bright sun was gone. Midnight-black clouds hung low over rooftops—not clouds at all but smoke that infused the air with a cloying cedar-y incense. I could no longer hear the helicopters that buzzed overhead for days. All along the lane, back doors slammed and garage doors opened, dogs barked, children chattered questions, parents murmured replies in calm voices. Cell phones rang, footsteps ran up and down back stairs, car engines started. I could not see over the fences but I could hear my neighbour, father of the two boys who had been playing minutes earlier. I called over the fence to him to make sure he knew of the voluntary evacuation. He was already loading his family into their big blue truck.

My neighbours on the other side were not home. They had two large dogs, a black-and-tan German shepherd we had named Mr. Barker,

and a black Labrador retriever we called Lieutenant Wooferson, pronouncing it "Leff-tenant" in the British way because we thought it was funny. The dogs were always outside and always barking, although not that day. It's something I have thought often about. I hoped they were away with their owners although for months I could not bring myself to ask.

Our detached double-car garage was at the back of our house and opened onto a rear laneway. It was insulated and heated in the winter, like most outbuildings in Fort McMurray. In the late spring, when we first arrived in town, a heated garage seemed a luxury. After our first winter, and our first experience of minus forty degrees, it seemed sane. Like most people, we kept the car stocked with booster cables and an extension cord to plug our block heater into the electrical outlets that dot local parking lots. We had also recently started locking the back door to the garage even when at home because there was a nearby break-in, the first neighbourhood crime since we moved in.

I unlocked the back door of the garage and reached for the rear hatch of our CRV. Our trunk was a jumble of reusable grocery bags, a common occurrence in McMurray and seen as a measure of how long you've been in town. Years before, the municipal council passed an environmental bylaw forbidding stores from selling disposable plastic bags. People grumbled but were proud that an oil town had an environmental standard that larger cities struggled to match. On the practical side, people forgot their bags in the car while shopping, usually when the temperature hovered between minus thirty-five and minus forty, so new bags were purchased again and again. After four years, we had more than thirty bags. That day, by force of habit, I started to carefully fold them.

"What the hell am I doing?" I thought, sweeping the pile onto the cement floor. I reached in and carefully removed Steve's camera tripod, still in the car after we used it to photograph the fire now headed towards me. After depositing the Go Bag and the bowl of keys

in the trunk, I left the hatch open and dashed across the deck and back into the kitchen, where my phone rang in my pocket.

"Did you open the garage door?" Steve asked.

"I unlocked it and started loading the car," I said.

"I mean the large one in front," he said. "Open it now in case the power goes out. The manual override is hard to tug open and the cord might be too high for you to reach."

"Right," I said.

"Pull out and shut the garage door against the smoke," Steve said. "You can load up at the front of the house."

"Right," I said.

I pivoted in the centre of the kitchen, turning back to the garage, and my eye caught a wicker basket beside our china cabinet. Already moving towards the door, I reached into the basket and, like a runner snatching a baton in an Olympic relay race, grasped the smooth, well-worn handle of a rolling pin that had belonged to Steve's late father. Reaching the car, I tucked the rolling pin behind the Go Bag where it wouldn't bang around. I slammed the hatch shut and jumped into the driver's seat. I eased into the laneway, looking carefully back and forth for traffic, the already forgotten camera tripod left nestled in a nest of reusable bags as I closed the garage door behind me.

As I pulled the car to the front of the house, I saw cars and trucks along our street, some double parked, trunks and hatches open. Every bit of curb space was occupied with the exception of a space directly in front of our house. As I nudged into the spot, neighbours ran in and out of their homes, dumping containers into their cars, suitcases and plastic bags and laundry hampers.

Two young Newfoundlanders, in their mid-twenties and staying with extended family next door, jogged down their front steps and along the little path to the front gate, dodging tricycles and toy trucks. I didn't know their names; they were new to town, part of the revolving work force. They wore brown work pants, blue work shirts and yellow steel-toed work boots despite the heat of the day, either just back from

a shift or having awakened from sleep ready to step into the clothes they planned to wear to work.

"What's after happenin' now?" said the blond man.

"The evacuation's up from voluntary to mandatory," said his companion. He had his cell phone in one hand, eyeing it as he spoke. "We gots fifteen minutes to blow."

"Beggars fricking belief," the blond man said, shaking his head.

They wished me well as they tossed their oversized canvas duffle bags into the trunk of the small blue car they had driven to Alberta from Newfoundland. They slowly pulled away from the curb, the driver looking over his shoulder to check for cars, his passenger looking at his phone.

I went back through the front door, which opened into our living room, and looked around for important, irreplaceable objects to stuff in the car.

It seemed odd that the first thing I picked up on my way out the door was a rolling pin. We had some relatively valuable family items, things my late father-in-law had loved, which I did not take. His favourite dress wristwatch, which Steve wore to work most days but, for no particular reason, had not that morning. A German-made wall clock that still tolled the hours with a melodic chime and which must have been an extravagance for Steve's grandparents. A bronze menorah by a well-known Jewish sculptor, the figures of Genesis intricately cast along the base and flowing out into the stems. A bronze and marble bust of my father-in-law's handsome head, an art piece so heavy I could not have carried it to the car. Two family treasures my father-in-law cherished were, providentially, away from the house because we had sent them out to be framed. One was a paper-thin, off-white prayer scarf given to him by the Dalai Lama. The other was the Member of the Order of Canada medal he was awarded in 1994.

That my father-in-law had such an eclectic collection of mementoes was not surprising. There was a time when discussions on

Canadian spiritual issues would inevitably point to his work. My father-in-law, Roy Bonisteel, was well-known to a generation of Canadians who grew up watching him host the Canadian Broadcasting Corporation's flagship television program on spirituality, an hour-long interview and documentary program called *Man Alive*.

People watching Roy's weekly programs saw a tall, well-spoken, patrician-looking man with a thick head of prematurely white hair. He wore a suit well, in the studied manner of a boy who grew up with one pair of hand-me-down shoes. He was charming and quick to smile, an active listener who focused on the person speaking as if they were the only one in the room. Roy interviewed the great spiritual thinkers and leaders of his day—Archbishop Desmond Tutu, the Dalai Lama, Mother Teresa, Jean Vanier, Elie Wiesel, to name a few. Roy, so the governor general said when he gave him his Order of Canada, had "come to symbolize integrity and decency to Canadians because of his personal unrelenting commitment to justice and humankind."

Why did I take his old rolling pin? It wasn't because my eye landed on it; I swept past many reminders of Roy as I ran through the house: paintings, photographs, certificates, jewelry, dozens of memories of a life well lived. The menorah, given to him by the artist to celebrate an early television program on Israel, was next to the front door and I dashed by it several times. But the truth was, when I thought of Roy, I pictured him rolling pie dough.

Roy retired as a fulltime broadcaster the year I met Steve but continued to write and work. He also made the rounds of the Canadian speaking circuit, where his favourite observation often found its way into his speeches: "We are moulded into a materialist world where we do a lot of eating, drinking and making merry until we ask the basic questions: 'Who am I? Where am I going? What is our purpose in life?'" Long before phrases like "eat, pray, love" entered the popular lexicon, Roy was practising what he preached about the interconnect-edness of material and spiritual well-being—happy to make merry, eat

and drink, while he explored the meaning of existence, his metaphysic-
al meanderings deeply rooted in the kitchen that was the centre of
his home.

Over the years, I came to know Roy's kitchen as well as my own.
I knew where he kept everything, his favourite over-sized, stainless
steel stirring spoon, which teapot was for green tea and which for
orange pekoe, the type of flour he preferred for bread and where he
kept the Tabasco sauce for his homemade Bloody Marys.

We cooked and talked, weaving back-and-forth, long, unhurried
conversations on a tapestry of topics. Spices (Roy advised going heavy
on them), the use of commas (Roy advised going light on them).
Spirituality (heavy), organized religion (light). Detective books (heavy
on character, light on violence). Crossword puzzles (*The Globe and
Mail*). Stain remover (white vinegar). The best writer on the search
for life's meaning (Holocaust survivor Viktor Frankl).

When it came to pie, Roy followed the seasons, starting with rhubarb,
then strawberry, then berries and fruits as they ripened throughout
the summer, ending with his favourite: apple. He was fussy about the
cheese he served with apple pie. His favourite brother-in-law was a
master cheesemaker who trained him in the squeakiness of fresh cheese
curds and proper storage for aging cheddar. (Good cheese turned out
to be something we longed for after we moved to Fort McMurray,
where there is no cheese factory, let alone a dairy cow, for hundreds
of kilometres.)

Roy made his pie crust the old-fashioned way, with lard and by
hand. He had to feel the dough in his hands to know he had the right
balance of salt and flour, and he had a special board for flouring and
rolling out crust. His movements were brisk and quick, like his moth-
er's on the farm when he was the youngest boy, helping her in the
kitchen while his father and siblings worked the fields. He had several
rolling pins he hung from a piece of driftwood in the living room
where they dangled precariously over his big brown leather couch.
(I am amazed that no one's skull was ever split open while we sat

beneath them watching the old movies he loved). Each of the rolling pins had its purpose and I knew which one was the best for pie crust. That was the one I lifted out of the basket as I went out the door.

A little over a foot long from the end of one handle to the other, the rolling pin is older than I am. Like the now-lost German clock, it had been a fixture in Roy's family farmhouse as long as he could remember. It is made of beech wood, now dark brown and well-seasoned from constant handling and natural oils. It was one of the few kitchen items Roy did not casually toss in the dishwasher. After each use, he wiped it with a warm cloth and hung it back on its precarious hook. Smaller than the usual rolling pin, it has a light heft that is good for my small hands. It whirled in Roy's big hands like a toy and he skimmed it over the pie dough with the economy of movement of a farm wife with mouths to feed. He never had to look while he did it and never missed a step, even if he was looking me in the eye as he made a point about the Buddhist path to liberation or papal infallibility or his sister Flossie's description of the local Orange Lodge marching in the Saint Patrick's Day parade.

Roy would work the dough, then wrap it tightly in plastic wrap and chill it for an hour, never touching it until it was ready. While we waited, we would slice apples or clean berries, and talk more. When the time was right, Roy rolled out the dough. It was always smooth and elastic, exactly the right amount and puffed up in the oven to the perfect height.

I never learned to make pie, not the way Roy made it. For one thing, I didn't like the idea of lard, which is rendered pig fat. Roy was one of the few people I met who had rendered a pig. On the farm his family used every part of the hog, hooves to tail. As a boy, he stood over a boiling fire and stirred the pot of fat trimmed during butchering. To keep it from burning as it melted down to the liquid form, the fat had to be stirred constantly for hours, a good job for the youngest person on a working farm. After the fat liquefied, it was set aside to form a solid, almost creamy, layer with water and impurities sinking to the bottom.

Roy's family used lard to make pastry and also for frying the meat they raised and the vegetables they grew. Sometimes for a quick breakfast they smeared lard on a piece of the homemade bread his mother baked every day in the wood stove.

Forget rendering lard. Even with store-bought lard, I didn't have the patience for Roy's hands-on approach to pie dough.

"I'm pretty busy, Roy," I said. "Isn't there a quicker way?"

"The real trick," Roy told me, "is to know when to stop working the dough. You can warm it too much with your hands."

"That's the trick all right," I said.

"It's practice and patience," said Roy. "There are no shortcuts."

The truth was, I would rather eat pie Roy baked than learn to do it myself. Roy was fine with that, partly because he knew his pies were excellent and partly because he was the kind of guy who let you get where you needed to go in your own time.

"I'll mull that over," I said.

"Don't overthink it," Roy said. "Just commit."

I was finally about to take Roy's advice as I packed up to flee the wildfire coming for my home. It wasn't until a week later I realized I had taken his rolling pin and left behind, on a shelf filled with four generations of family photos, the sealed wooden box containing Roy's cremated ashes.

4 | THE PLASTER SAINT

A BLUE PLASTIC BOX sat empty at the foot of our stairs. I had dropped it on the bottom step after carting papers from my second-storey home office to the recycling bin. A few months after the fire, I borrowed a measuring tape to gauge its size because my sister Annette, who was storing items I had saved from the fire, said she didn't think I needed much shelf space.

"That box is a lot smaller than you remember," Annette said.

She was right. It was about the size of two loaves of bread.

The box seemed larger as I knelt before a brown mission-style bric-a-brac shelf in our living room and dropped family treasures into it. They were mostly small items. A photograph. Brass bells. For a second, my hand hovered over a foot-high plaster statue of Saint Therese.

At that point, I expected to be allowed home the next day. That happened during the 2013 flood evacuation, not to mention over the weekend in nearby neighbourhoods, where mandatory evacuations had been ordered and then rescinded within twenty-four hours. Saint Therese was fragile and the odds were low that she would survive a bumpy trip. It might be better to leave her safely on her shelf. But I

25

decided to take her and tucked her in the box. I nestled her inside one of Steve's sweaters and tucked her between the old snapshot of a favourite pet and the antique bells.

I was experiencing the telescoping effect that people describe in moments of stress, my vision tunnelled to the items in front of me. I watched my hands reach out and select objects and put them in the box. I thought, "What a pile of old junk." I doubt anything in the box was worth more than fifty bucks. I kept packing. My breathing was loud. My mouth was dry. My heart raced. Sweat trickled down my back. I decided the box was full.

I speed-walked to the car holding the box in both hands, perching it carefully on the roof while I opened the door, then slipped it into the back seat. I ran back in for other items I stacked around it, some family books, an old award, another sweater. I reopened the hatch and loaded two guitars in their cases, a mirror and a framed needlepoint. I tossed a final armload of items into the passenger's seat, including my purse, climbed in and closed the driver's door.

Along the street, doors and trunks slammed and engines turned over. I was used to hearing country and western songs blare from speakers when cars started but there was no music. As I took in the quickly emptying street it hit me that, after four years of insisting the post-apocalyptic depiction of Fort McMurray was a myth, here was a scene out of a Hollywood movie where residents flee a tornado, an earthquake, a killer comet.

I put the key in the ignition, then paused to take a last look at the house and noticed the open window in the upstairs bedroom. I knew what the smoke damage from one open window could mean. I ran back up my front walk, unlocked the front door, clicked off the alarm, and ran back inside. I dashed up the stairs and into the bedroom, past the neatly made bed. Past family photos from the Chapeau, Québec, county fair lined along a bench made from wood hewn from Steve's family farm. Past the oversized stack of books by my bedside table, a stack that never decreased because I added books as fast as I read

them. Past the watercolour of juggling vaudevillians, an artist rendering of one of my published short stories.

Smoke poured in through the two-inch opening in the window. The burning boreal forest smelled like an enormous campfire, not yet the toxic-garbage stink of burning houses. The low-hanging smoke was the same inky black as the ubiquitous ravens who provided the cawing soundtrack of McMurray. I realized with a start that the huge, fearless birds had flown away. The street below was almost deserted as I wound the knob to shut the window, snapping shut the catches and tightly sealing it, then pulling down the thick wooden blinds.

As I left the bedroom, I had an image of Steve and me sleeping on cots in an evacuation shelter, covered by wool blankets. Why that image came to me while I sweated in the heat, I will never know. I am allergic to wool so I opened the hallway linen closet and reached for the top shelf and a quilt my mother-in-law gave us on our last visit to Ontario. As I stood on my tip toes and reached for it, I knocked over linens from lower shelves and started to pick them up and refold them, then realized I would have time for that when the evacuation ended— or they would burn with the house. I dragged the quilt from its high shelf, trailing it behind me as I ran out the door.

I threw the quilt into the back seat where I could find it later if we needed it at the shelter and sent Steve a quick text that I was heading out. I expected to meet him in ten minutes, the usual time required for a leisurely drive to his workplace. Almost alone on the street, I looked carefully over my shoulder, rolled cautiously onto the roadway and turned right.

For the first sixty seconds, it was a normal trip along Athabasca Drive. The street gently meanders the two-kilometre length of our neighbourhood, ending at a four-way stop at the top of Abasand Hill, where all traffic in the subdivision converges on a divided four-lane road that is the only exit. To get there, I had to drive the entire length of our neighbourhood.

I had driven the route hundreds of times. Usually, in the early afternoon of a weekday, I would see a dozen people out and about, watering lawns, unloading groceries or pushing baby strollers as they walked to the mailbox. At any time of day or night, shift workers slumbered in bedrooms around the community.

Driveways and front lawns were filled with scurrying people stowing suitcases, laundry hampers, plastic bins and diaper bags into trucks and vans and cars. Children clutching stuffed animals and juice boxes were buckled into car seats. Pet carriers were crammed in back seats beside food and water dishes, bags of dog chow and cat litter. All along the road people pulled out of driveways and the traffic slowed. It came to a dead stop, ironically, by the cemetery where tiny flags and plastic flowers dotted the tidy graves.

After fifteen minutes at a standstill, I turned off the car's engine. If, after I made it to Steve's workplace, we were forced to head north to Firebag—an oil sands work camp two hundred kilometres north where I knew the next round of evacuation centres would be—there were no gas stations. This, I later found out, turned out to be one of the most practical decisions I made that day. It not only saved gas, it meant my car engine was not sucking in the smoke and ashes that could knock it out and stall me in my tracks.

I watched a family crawl over their home, a man on the roof, a woman by the front veranda, soaking the shingles and the siding with garden hoses. Two girls tossed pillowcases that looked stuffed full of clothing into the back seat of a brown car sitting with its doors open. I had lots of time to watch, because the traffic didn't move.

When the friendly Newfoundlanders told me earlier that the voluntary evacuation was upgraded to mandatory, I put it down to muddled communication, assuming it was supposed to be mandatory all along. Now I assumed there had been another communications glitch at the Emergency Ops Centre and the Royal Canadian Mounted Police had not been directed to the intersection ahead.

I have a strict no-phone policy when driving but I was parked so I took out my cell. Based on my emergency training, I knew social media would be confusing and misinformation flowing freely. I would get my information from Steve, who should have been getting it directly from the Emergency Ops Centre so he could post it on the City website. I texted him about the need for RCMP to get the traffic moving.

'Don't panic,' Steve texted back.

"What the hell?" I thought. In the thirty years I had known Steve, he had never once, not ever, told me not to panic.

'Why should I panic?' I texted.

'No reason,' he replied.

'Are you panicking?' I texted.

'Forget I said that,' he replied. 'I can see the intersection. The RCMP are there. Shouldn't be long.'

I should have realized something was horribly wrong. But panicking never occurred to me. Even though I moved barely fifty metres in thirty minutes. Even though each time the line moved, it was by a single car length. Even though the car's air conditioning abruptly quit, surprising because we had the car in for a tune-up two weeks before and everything was fine. It was nearly thirty-four degrees now and turning on the car fan meant blowing even hotter air over myself, so it was easier to leave everything turned off as I conserved gas. I kept the windows rolled up against the smoke. I wondered if changing into my jeans had been such a good idea.

With the windows rolled up, there was little communication along the line of vehicles, especially with everyone staying in our cars to be ready when the line moved. Ash drifted down like dandelion fluff on a summer day. I flipped the dial to local radio stations but heard only pre-recorded music. It can't be that bad, I thought, or they would be broadcasting live.

Everyone on Athabasca Drive sat patiently in the long, snaking row and left the incoming lane clear for emergency vehicles. An

ambulance raced into the neighbourhood, lights flashing and siren blaring. It cut through the middle of the line, a few cars in front of me, and waiting vehicles inched over to make room as it pulled down a cul-de-sac. Paramedics pushing a stretcher raced into a home, running up the steps of the veranda and almost immediately racing back out holding up an oxygen tank and a patient strapped under a long white sheet. They folded the stretcher flat like an ironing board and slid it into the back of the ambulance, the rear doors slamming shut. Family members jumped into a car parked out front and the two vehicles sped through the space left in the line for their exit. They headed out down the incoming lane, lights and sirens blaring to warn oncoming traffic.

For a brief moment, I thought about pulling out of traffic and following them, jumping the queue. But I was alone, no one was depending on me to get them to safety, so I decided to wait my turn. Only one vehicle, a large pickup, pulled out from our line to follow as the ambulance cleared a path.

Sitting between two bends in the road, I had no idea what was happening ahead. Our long line of cars sat patiently, some with engines running and some not. Some gas tanks were close to empty. I saw people in driveways and garages draining gasoline from ATVs and lawn mowers and snowmobiles. People parked in front and behind me siphoned gas from recreational vehicles they towed on trailers.

From where I sat, I could, for the most part, see the office building where Steve worked. From the web browser on my phone I could tell he was on the job, sending out emergency messages for the munici-pality. I knew if the word went out for the people in that line along Athabasca Drive to abandon their cars, Steve would be one of the first people to get that word. If he didn't hear from me, he would come get me. It sounds melodramatic—movie-of-the-week—but I knew it.

I looked for a clear path down the Abasand Hill across Highway 63 to the Clearwater River on the east side of the downtown core. I watched several people on foot head down the hill carrying large, overstuffed backpacks. They were not running and did not seem panicked. I

assumed they didn't have cars and, with no buses operating, were walking to the evacuation shelter at the north end of the downtown. The packs looked heavy. If I had to run for it, I decided, I would carry nothing but my purse with my identification and my phone.

I had been treadmill running every day for the past six months, training for a five-kilometre run I hoped to do that summer with my sister. I was pretty sure I could make it to the river if I had to, even in the smoke. I would have to be very careful crossing the highway. I would look both ways and listen hard for traffic so I didn't get run over by a fire truck. I made sure my car doors were unlocked. I double-checked my purse with my identification and put it on the seat beside me. I took a deep breath of the smoky air inside the car. I watched ash drift down from the sky to land on the windshield and I turned on the windshield wipers to brush it aside.

I know how it sounds. I thought Steve would give me advance warning. I thought I would out-run a raging forest fire. I thought Steve would find me in the smoke and the chaos. But if flames appeared around the bend in the road ahead, I was going to give it a hell of a good try.

While I mulled over my plan, the line inched slowly forward, one car space at a time. The afternoon sky grew blacker, the smoke hung lower. The white ash fell faster. The heat grew more intense. I lost all sense of wind direction; the smoke was everywhere and the ash seemed to fall straight down. I started to get thirsty but had tossed the small bag with food and water into the trunk and I didn't want to get out into the smoke to get it in case the line started moving more quickly.

News was spilling out across the country about the fire because there were already reporters in town to cover the evacuation ordered over the weekend. As I sat in the parked car, I started to get emails and texts and phone calls. At first people checked in with a mild concern, assuming I was well away from the action. I tried to be reassuring but truthful and as people found out I was evacuating on the one route out of my neighbourhood, the tone of the messages changed. Don't worry, I told people. As soon as the snafus I was sure were happening at the

Emergency Ops Centre were resolved, traffic would start moving along more smoothly.

At one point my phone beeped to signal an email from Ontario about some personal business, something that seemed important. I wanted to wait a day or two to formulate a response and dashed off a quick reply to the woman working with me.

"I can't talk now," I told her. "My neighbourhood is under a mandatory evacuation order from a wildfire."

She replied immediately. "Are you safe?"

"Absolutely," I assured her. "Fires happen all the time in the north. It's just a precaution. This is the third or fourth neighborhood evacuation this month."

She emailed back: no problem, they had extended the deadline and I could take my time.

In her office, she turned on the news to see images from McMurray. The reporters were being evacuated from point to point just ahead of the flames, filing breathless stories whenever they had a chance to stop.

She emailed again: "Are you sure you're okay?"

"I'm fine," I responded. "It won't be long now. I'll be safe soon."

"If you don't mind," she responded, "I'm going to pray for you."

"That would be nice," I answered, but I was taken aback. I never thought of myself as the kind of person who needed prayers. I thought of myself as the type of the person who helped answer them.

She replied one last time. "Please let me know when you are safe. Email any time, day or night."

"I will," I promised. "Don't worry. It's almost over."

"Holy crap," I thought as I put the phone on the passenger seat beside me. "How bad is this if people on the other side of the country are praying for me?"

Then I thought of the plaster saint in the box in the back seat.

I'd had been lugging that saint around for more than forty years. My Canadian grandmother, Madeleine Hawkins Greenwood, had left it to

me in a codicil to her will, a handwritten list on lined yellow notepaper that listed the names of her four dozen grandchildren. Next to each name was a gift she wanted them to receive after her death.

They were small gifts, none worth a great deal of money, and everybody got something. I think my sisters Kim and Annette got some costume jewelry that our grandmother wore to church and weddings. My sister Cathy got an antique bone china teacup. It had delicate red roses hand-painted on both sides and was trimmed in gold leaf. It sat for years on a special top shelf at my grandparents' home. As far as I know, no tea was ever sipped from it and it did not have a single chip.

Saint Therese had seen better days. It was the standard version of the statue that you see in churches around the world. She stands in a contemplative pose, eyes modestly downcast, dressed in the brown and cream habit of the Carmelite religious order. These days such statues are made of resin but this one was an old-fashioned plaster saint. When my grandfather handed her to me after his wife's death, her paint was faded and chipped, with chunks of plaster showing through her long cape. The tip of her nose was gone; so was the toe of the shoe peeking from under her hem. The roses she nestled to her chest were faded brown lumps indistinguishable from the plain cross in their midst. Her head had once fallen off, but my grandmother had stuck it back on with Scotch Tape. Through the yellowing tape, which I hadn't removed in case her whole head disintegrated, was one buttugly Saint Therese.

My knowledge of saints is spotty, although there were books about saints lying around our Catholic school, where I read everything I could get my hands on. I've forgotten most of the stories, except for a gruesome rip-snorter about Father Damien and the lepers, with bad guys and a plague and a dramatic ending. Saint Therese's story, which was in the same book, was not a rip-snorter. She joined a cloister and offered up her daily tasks to God. She scrubbed a lot of floors, which was something I could picture because I helped my mother scrub

floors for summer cottagers. She was bullied at school, and that I had no trouble picturing. But I had no interest in offering any suffering up to God. I preferred old-fashioned smiting of the evildoers.

I had been dragging around my plaster saint for years. Long after I said goodbye to my childhood collection of *Black Stallion* books bought with money from house cleaning and babysitting, the Avon charm bracelet my godmother had given me, and a gold ring from my late Aunt Corey, there was the broken-headed Saint Therese. It's hard for someone raised as a Catholic to toss out icons. I have seen friends clean out their late parents' house to find themselves left with a collection of crucifixes, holy water bottles, Bibles, and rosaries that looks like a vampire-killing kit.

The Scotch-Taped saint was still sitting atop one of my bookshelves when, after seeing the writing on the wall for the newspaper business, I answered an ad for a communications director for an order of Roman Catholic women religious. Unlike Saint Therese, they were not "nuns" who belonged to a contemplative order behind closed walls, but "Sisters" who did social justice work in the community. At that time, they were protesting cuts to social assistance programs for groups with whom they had been working for more than a century.

One of the Sisters was an artist who created nativity scenes, which she sold, donating the money to a soup kitchen. She offered to repair my statue and I was astonished at the miraculous resuscitation. Saint Therese's head was so well repaired I had to look closely for the cracks, the habit restored in cream and brown, roses bright red, her eyes shining. Now she smiled, looking down at her flowers with a contented appreciation. She looked better, I suspected, than when she arrived at Grandma Greenwood's house. Restored, she went onto the knick-knack shelf.

In northern Alberta, months before the fire, I had taken another look at Saint Therese. I had travelled to Fort Chipewyan, the northernmost town in the region, accessible by winter ice road or air. There, a local Indigenous woman had, with the generosity you find everywhere

in the north, spontaneously offered a tour of the Church of the Nativity of the Blessed Virgin Mary. It was a notorious building, formerly part of a residential school complex that included the tragically named Holy Angels residential school. Originally built on a stark rocky outcrop, the school has long since burned to the ground. The area retains the feel, as the woman told me, "of ghosts who cry at night."

The church, however, has been reclaimed as a community space. The building, a one-and-a-half-storey wood frame structure with double front doors and a bell tower, is lovingly cared for by community members, many of them survivors of the residential school system. The exterior is bright white despite weathering some of Canada's harshest weather. The inside is warm and light-filled, with bright blue murals on the ceiling done with berry juice and fish oil, walls salmon pink with green columns, the trim red and green with steady lines of gold. A natural altar made from local wood and polished to a high sheen fills the space. As a symbol of renewal and rejuvenation, it is powerful and, unfortunately, rare. It's a physical manifestation of endurance and grace—and in one corner was a familiar face.

"I see my old friend, Saint Therese," I said. She sat in her own alcove to the right of the natural wood altar, larger but otherwise identical to my grandmother's plaster saint.

"Yes," said the woman. "She's our friend, too."

I needed a friend as I sat alone in the long line of cars between two bends in the road. I didn't know just how badly. On the southern end of Abasand, a few hundred metres away from where I sat parked, homes were burning. RCMP officers and firefighters were desperately racing to get families out of the neighbourhood and down the sharply curving road to the highway. Vehicles were escaping through the main intersection—the only exit—which was why those of us on the northern end of the subdivision were not moving.

When I finally rounded the last bend on Athabasca Drive, I saw bedlam at the four-way stop at the top of the hill. Usually a divided road with two lanes inbound and two outbound, all traffic flowed out,

vehicles moving one car space at a time. A lone fire engine, lights flashing but no siren, was slowly driving up the shoulder of the incoming lane, a woman firefighter walking in front to keep the path clear, other firefighters on foot alongside the engine.

Every person not in a vehicle was in uniform. They called to each other and to people in the cars, shouting and gesturing with large, broad motions. I rolled down my windows but I could make no sense of the cacophonic jumble of voices and engines and braking and acceleration. At the four-way stop, a young police constable without a breathing mask stood in the middle of the smoke-filled intersection. Traffic came towards him from three directions. He twisted continually, watching adrenaline-fueled drivers steadily creeping forward though the chaos.

I hesitated for a moment as my turn came at the four-way stop, confused and worried about smashing into someone or something and bringing everything to a stop. My head swivelled back and forth. I saw more people with overstuffed knapsacks jogging down the roadside on the long grass, passing on the far side of the fire engine coming up the shoulder. They were heading straight for the highway and the evacuation centre that had been opened over the weekend in a recreation facility on the other side of the Snye River. They would have to dash across the smoke-filled highway, then cross two kilometres of the downtown to reach it.

The frantic motioning of the young constable urged me to pull across traffic into the far-left lane, which I realized I needed to be in to get to Steve. Most of the traffic was heading south and to Edmonton, but I needed to head north into the city centre where he waited.

The traffic started moving in my lane, still a car length at a time, but faster. Now I was moving, it occurred to me I should take a photograph with my new cell phone. But there was no stopping. After the long wait, I was gliding along on the road to Steve's office and there were no cars in front of me. My goal had been to get out of our neighbourhood and to make it to Steve. I had done it, I thought. It was over.

In the back of my car, nestled in her blue plastic bed, my tenderly repaired Saint Therese was still in one piece, shaken but unbroken. She had a long way to travel before the night was over.

5 | THE SLEIGH BELLS

ON WARM DAYS, McMurray's downtown is packed with people claiming a place in the summer sun. The lower town site, as it is known, has its own parks and trails, its eastern edge stretching along the Clearwater River, which flows north to meet the Athabasca River. The previous summer, I spent a lazy afternoon sitting by the bench of a visiting college soccer team, out-of-town rivals from the biggest school in Edmonton, watching them grow increasingly perturbed as the local team outplayed them. The home team's efforts were boosted by loud cheers from families enjoying a fine day. Enormous baby strollers dotted the sidelines, and the smell of sunscreen wafted through the air. Fans sat side by side in portable lawn chairs decorated with Canadian flags, halter-top-wearing mothers with expensively inked sleeve tattoos sitting next to mothers in bright hijabs, designer sunglasses and sparkling sneakers.

McMurray's multicultural landscape is most obvious in the downtown. You hear three or four different languages when picking up a prescription at the drug store, getting off the bus at the mall or waiting at the post office where parcels arrive from all over the world. The

city's diversity encourages a nonchalant generosity, often demonstrated by young mothers busy with work and young children. When I first moved to town, I announced at a marketing event that I missed small family-run restaurants, cost prohibitive in the north given the high commercial rents. The next day my co-workers brought me containers of home-cooked food, vindaloo and chana masala and cod tongues, sharing recipes as well as instructions for where to buy ingredients. Steve and I started frequenting the grocery store's world food section, with sauces, teas, rice, beans and spices in greater supply than we were used to in southeastern Ontario.

Across from the world food aisle, a freezer was devoted to large seven-pound plastic buckets of salt beef used to make Jiggs Dinner. It's a traditional Newfoundland meal of turnip, cabbage, potato, carrots, bread pudding, pease pudding, boiled in one pot with the salt beef and then smothered with gravy on platter-sized plates. We became regular customers of the Newfoundland restaurant that served it every Thursday, Steve manfully finishing his portion while I ate only the vegetables coated with salty grease, leaving the salt beef in the middle of the platter and prompting one friend to call me "the world's worst vegetarian." We were never tempted by the menu's other popular Newfoundland meal, a "Mess" of wieners, bologna, cheese, bread stuffing, and enough gravy to choke your arteries and those of the person sitting next to you. Inside on a winter's day, you could have been in downtown St. John's with waitresses calling you "my love" and patrons announcing, "This gravy better be some hot or someone will know it, by Jesus." As I drove along Franklin Street, the Newfoundland restaurant, which only closed on Christmas Day, was shut down, its windows dark, the parking lot empty.

The next empty parking lot was at the Tim Hortons coffee shop and it was a shocking sight. On my first day in town I queued there for thirty minutes, dwarfed by huge men in the ubiquitous reflective vests and work boots, all ordering large "double-doubles"—the two-creams-and-two-sugars coffee order often the first bit of Canadian slang

picked up by newcomers to the country. On my first visit, the drive-through line held thirty cars, which I learned was typical at any time of day or night. The Tim Hortons was so busy it became the flashpoint for an issue the rest of Alberta thought ended with the oil boom—the need for temporary foreign workers. The federal government's decision to place a moratorium on new temporary foreign workers left the McMurray service sector struggling to find employees, the program an important first step for many seeking to become new Canadians.

That had been the path for one of my friends, a hair stylist, whom I did not see until weeks later, when the evacuation orders were finally lifted. The story he told me was typical of the hundreds I heard post-fire, an ordinary working day interrupted by catastrophic circumstances. My friend had just finished applying a full treatment of hair dye when the downtown evacuation order was announced. He calmly rinsed out the dye, reassured his client that he would not abandon her with harsh chemicals soaking into her scalp, carefully drying and combing out her hair before she left the salon. While I was driving empty streets towards Steve's office, my friend locked up the salon to emerge into a smoke-darkened city where buses no longer ran and flames were visible along the hill bordering the downtown. He raced through numbers in his cell phone to find everyone he knew was already on the road, many stuck in traffic jams in other parts of town. Finally, he located a colleague waiting to fuel up a few blocks away and sprinted to the gas station, jumping into the back seat of the car with nothing but what he had taken to work with him that morning.

I had been expecting a downtown filled with emergency vehicles, flashing lights and screaming sirens; my brain wasn't processing that the streets were deserted except for a few lost souls headed on foot for the homeless shelter across from City Hall. I drove past Steve's workplace, even though there were plenty of parking spaces, to pull into the usual parking lot almost two blocks away. Always filled during the work day, the lot was empty. It was, I realized as I stepped out of my car, unnervingly quiet. There were no car engines idling or satellite

radios playing, no buses rumbling by, no voices. The ravens were gone, too, no cawing or scuffling around garbage bins. I could hear the rubber soles of my sneakers plopping on the dusty sidewalk as I jogged to City Hall, my small cloth purse rubbing against my hip, the car keys jingling in my hand. The air was thick with wood smoke and sweat dripped between my shoulder blades. I thought about going back to the car and moving it closer but I wasn't turning around. I decided to get to Steve—and that was the last decision I wanted to make on my own.

Steve came down from his sixth-floor office to let me in, opening a door at the rear of the building and giving me a quick hug.

"I didn't panic," I said.

"Where's the car?" he said.

"In the usual lot," I said.

"We need to move it closer," he said.

"I noticed there are no cars," I said. "Where is everyone?"

"The downtown has been evacuated," he said.

"What?"

"Everyone is evacuated from City Hall," he said, "but I need to post a last update on the website."

For once I didn't say that if I was the Public Information Officer I would have based my web guy at the Emergency Operations Centre, about ten kilometres away on the south end of town. Steve was the web guy. If he was at the Ops Centre, he would have been stranded there without a vehicle. With the traffic rerouting and roads closing, I would not have been able to make it there to pick him up. Instead he was standing beside me.

We walked to the car together and I babbled on, describing what I had seen in Abasand, blurting out questions. Steve told me what he knew from the emergency communications he posted online. The downtown evacuation shelter was closed. The hospital was shutting down and patients being evacuated, the most serious ones airlifted to Edmonton. The radio stations were evacuated, the programming on a continuous loop. The Waterways neighbourhood was being

evacuated. Gregoire might be on fire. Beacon Hill—between Abasand and Gregoire—was on fire.

We moved the car to the foot of the City Hall building and went back in so Steve could keep working. We decided that, having only one vehicle, I would wait in his office so we could leave together. As we got to Steve's desk and he logged onto his computer, I found myself thinking of him as the last telegraph operator on the Titanic, dutifully sending signals into the ether while the lifeboats filled up.

Then, despite everything I had just learned about the fire, I found myself relaxing. The electricity was on and the air conditioning inside the building was working. The air inside the sealed building did not smell of smoke. Sweat stopped trickling down my back and for the first time in hours I was comfortable. I took deep breaths and felt some of the tension leave my neck. I flexed my fingers, my hands sore from how tightly I had gripped the steering wheel. I slumped in my chair and ate an apple leftover from Steve's lunch, not because I was hungry but because I was afraid of getting a headache if I didn't take in some nutrients.

There was nothing for me to do and I felt unsettled. All of my training had been geared to working in an emergency, keeping public safety information flowing to the community, making decisions, helping people. I finished the apple and put the core in a garbage can where it probably sat for weeks, one of the thousands of pieces of rotting fruit that would greet people when the re-entry phase began.

The municipality's chief administrative officer, pale and worried, came into Steve's office. He was checking each floor of City Hall to make sure it was empty, like a pilot going down the line of seats in the cabin to make sure everyone had escaped a crash-landed aircraft. He told us to get out as soon as Steve posted the information and that he would wait in the lobby to make sure we left. Steve finished his posting and packed up his work laptop, carefully checking for power cords and connectors, knowing he would be working throughout the emergency. I took Steve's lunch bag and its few leftover snacks. We left behind

his thermos because he had already finished the coffee he brewed at home that morning. We should have filled it with drinking water from the fountain because we were about to spend hours in a hot car with a now-broken air conditioner.

When Steve and I got to the first floor, the chief administrative officer and the mayor were standing in the lobby between the two main exits. Mayor Melissa Blake, a woman with whom I have worked closely and whom I respect and admire, is a well-put-together figure of poise and grace. Even though she had two young boys who were being evacuated, she was at her post. She looked worried, her face drawn and her brows knit together.

"A captain is supposed to go down with the ship," she said as she took my hand. "Does that mean a mayor is supposed to go down with her City Hall?"

"I don't think there's an etiquette for this," I said.

"I suppose not," she said. Melissa would later call the fire a "multi-headed monster," evoking images of the mythical Cerberus, the dog who guards the gates of hell, or the predatory nine-headed Hydra, which grows two new heads each time one is cut off. Steve and I headed to the door, leaving her to her battle.

"Be safe," she said. "Good luck."

I wished her the same as Steve and I left through the back door, crossed the empty street and got into the car. It would be many hours and hundreds of kilometres before we left it again. We knew from the emergency information Steve had posted that the highway south to Edmonton was blocked by fire and crews were battling to reopen it. All traffic was being directed north towards the larger residential subdivisions, where people would stay with friends or family, or further north to evacuation shelters at oil industry sites. We decided to head to Dickinsfield, a neighbourhood on the northwestern edge of the city, and arranged to stay for what we thought would be a night or two.

Our young friend Ashley—who often joked Steve and I were her "work parents"—had contacted us as soon as she heard our neighbourhood

was being evacuated to offer the use of her condominium. We planned to stay there that night, store the possessions I had gathered, and get back to our home in the next day or so. We had to pick up her keys from a friend in Dickinsfield and travel to her nearby Timberlea condo, a matter of a few kilometres. We would have all the comforts of home for a few days. The worst we expected was a power outage because we knew there were only a few power lines carrying electricity and gas into the city, and those could be in the path of the fire.

I found myself wishing more than a few times that I had taken time in the previous two weeks to learn how to use my new phone. I had not bothered to embrace the technology literally at my fingertips, partly out of laziness and partly out of cussedness at being laid off and forced to transfer my contact list to a new system. I was still figuring out the basics and now, with Steve driving, I was juggling my phone and his while family and friends contacted us as news spread across the country. The national media coverage meant my phone's incoming-message alert, which I could not figure how to turn off, beeped constantly. I sent out what I thought were reassuring messages. However, I was mixing things up, answering one person's question with a response to a different person's account, reading emails out to Steve as he drove, and typing the wrong answer on the wrong phone.

It got serious as we grew closer to Dickinsfield and saw a wall of flames breaking along the road and heading towards the rows of well-appointed family homes. The fire had jumped the Athabasca River and was burning the southern slope of Fort McMurray's northern neighbourhoods. As Steve looked for the next intersection and a chance to turn out of the path of the fire, I texted Ashley urgently, something along the lines of: 'Tell your friend to get out. We can see flames. This is serious. We cannot get to her. Every car in Dickinsfield is on the road. She needs to get out.'

Except I sent the text to an out-of-province friend whom I had just assured everything was fine. Her reply was along the lines of, 'I think you have the wrong person but OH MY GOD.'

'Oops never mind, it's not that bad,' I lied. 'I was embellishing to make a point so the person would get moving'. Then I accidentally sent her another stop-fooling-around-and-get-the-hell-out text. I'm sure she didn't sleep a wink that night but she has never mentioned it.

It seemed to me, after I sat alone in the car for so long in Abasand, that we were soaring along at top speed. We left Steve's workplace on the tail end of the downtown evacuation and most of the traffic had cleared, allowing us to zip northbound to the subdivision and make good time towards Dickinsfield. Turning around, we were swallowed up in the mass exodus out of that neighbourhood. We crept towards Ashley's condo without her key, hoping another friend who lived in the building might be able to find us a way in, or at least store some of our items if we headed to a shelter. Maybe, our worst-case scenario, we could use Ashley's parking spot and sleep in the car.

At the same time, with local radio stations evacuated, the outside media was the only live news connection back into the community. Steve and I are long-time public radio listeners and for more than a decade I had been a regional correspondent for the Canadian Broadcasting Corporation. Years earlier, the massive ice storm that hit our home town in southeastern Ontario taught us to listen to the CBC for emergency updates. During the ice storm, local cell and broadcast towers crumpled, taking radio, television and cell phones out of commission. Regular telephone wires snapped under the weight of the ice, making land lines useless. With information and public safety a top priority, CBC Radio had used its transmitters and relay stations to boost its signal and reach out to people affected by the storm. Now we tuned to CBC Radio Edmonton, which had turned over all coverage to the fire. That was how we heard the entire city was being evacuated. Almost instantly, traffic began to swell into the streets from all directions. We headed towards the highway, usually a ten-minute drive at the busiest of times.

As we inched along for the next three hours we saw no signs of panic and very few of impatience. People waited their turn. They used

their signals. They obeyed the traffic rules, even at four-way stops. At one major intersection without stoplights a middle-aged woman stood in the middle of the road and directed traffic. She looked exhausted and overheated despite her shorts and flip-flops. She took sips from a water bottle as she waved to move cars through the intersection. She could have been inside packing her own household, as thousands of other people were doing. But she was preventing gridlock at a key location and adding a sense of order to chaos. I turned to wave to her as we moved through the intersection but she was already looking at the next car.

We crept on.

We were approaching our fourth hour of stop-and-go traffic and things were more stop than go. That's when we noticed that every time Steve stepped on the brakes, bells rang out.

"Am I starting to lose it?" Steve asked. "Do I hear sleigh bells?"

"Yes and yes," I said. "I packed my grandfather's sleigh bells."

"Smart thinking," Steve said. "Sleigh bells will come in handy today."

It was thirty-four degrees Celsius inside the car. The air conditioning had conked out in the first hour, but we kept the windows rolled up because the smoke was aggravating Steve's asthma. I had put his prescription puffer in my Go Bag but it was almost empty.

"I'll muffle them," I said.

We hadn't moved in fifteen minutes, so I hopped out, opened the door to the back seat and reached into the blue plastic tub and took out the sleigh bells. I cushioned the clappers on the bells against the leather seat to stifle the sound. They weren't the kind of bells kids shake at Christmas concerts. They were about one hundred years old and sat upright—three shiny brass bells on a black wrought-iron band designed to be mounted on the front of a horse-drawn sleigh. They were made to ring out in bad weather to let other people know you were heading towards them on a dark, narrow path.

The bells have a beautiful jingle, a long cheerful peal that echoes merrily before fading to a tinkle. Even on that hot, smoke-filled,

apocalyptic day, the sound brought to mind old-fashioned Christmases and my childhood home on Wolfe Island, which is—as Steve is fond of quoting because he has heard it repeated so often— "the largest of the Thousand Islands." It sits where the St. Lawrence River and Lake Ontario meet, with upper New York state and the hamlet of Cape Vincent to its south. To its north is Kingston, which claims to be Canada's first capital city. The Island is nearly eighteen kilometres long, eight kilometres wide and, according to its residents, the centre of the universe. The Greenwoods have been there since they were Boisverts—French Canadians who arrived in the nineteenth century to work in the area shipyards, both on the Canadian and American side, depending on who was paying more.

The bells also reminded me of my grandfather, Vincent Thomas Greenwood. My sisters and I were among Vincent's youngest grandchildren. In his late seventies when we were small, he was the caretaker at the town dump but spent only a few hours there each day so he had time to tell us the stories we adored.

Vincent's best stories were about his home and his family, and his narratives reached back into the early 1800s. When he was a boy, he said, his Québécois grandparents greeted him with *bonjour, mon petit bonhomme.* He told how he helped my great-grandfather Thomas haul sand by horse-drawn wagon to build the foundation for Sacred Heart of Mary Church. He told how my grandmother prayed a novena so he would fail the medical for conscription into World War I.

Our favourite story was about a runaway horse and wagon. We loved it because my grandfather was the central character. As a young man, he was training a colt to pull a wagon when the animal spooked and ran the entire length of the main street of the Island's only village, knocking over water barrels and flower pots, tearing through clotheslines and dodging other wagons. Somehow, no one was hurt. After bringing the colt under control, Vincent returned to the village where people asked if a runaway horse and wagon had raced past him. Naturally, he said no. He embellished the story with details about our

village (the two-storey clapboard houses, the limestone town hall, the post office and ferry dock) and funny descriptions of local characters (the storekeeper, the school teacher, the ferry captain and the priest).

My grandfather gave me the sleigh bells on one of my last visits. We shared a piece of the homemade pie my cousin always made for him—blueberry that week—and we ate it from small dessert plates as my grandfather, well into his nineties and a little breathless, again told me the old story of the runaway wagon. He rushed over words he had savoured in the past, no longer taking dramatic pauses, telling the story by rote. But after he recited his triumphant ending, he opened the cupboard under the kitchen sink and took out the sleigh bells and handed them to me. They were mine now, he said, because I loved that story so much.

After the fire, I repeated the story of the evacuation and our escape over and over. Like a lot of people in McMurray, I told funny stories about the objects I saved and the twists and turns of our trip out of town. We had careened past danger, saved by a full gas tank, comically hearing sleigh bells I had rescued on the hottest day of the year.

Weeks later, Steve and I were still marveling over the story of our escape when we sorted through what I had saved. We talked about a good friend with a well-appointed woodshop and wondered if he might make a wall rack from which we could hang the rolling pin. There was the plaster saint, too, still without a scratch, and we wondered if she would look lonely on a shelf with no books to surround her. I picked up the sleigh bells and a merry peal rang out, immediately taking me to a muggy, smoke-filled roadside and a backseat of jumbled mementoes.

"Am I starting to lose it?" I asked Steve. "Am I telling the story of our escape like it was my grandfather's runaway wagon?"

"Yes and yes," Steve said. "It's a good story."

"It has a happy ending," I said. "Doesn't it?"

"So far, so good," said Steve. "Let's see what happens."

6 | THE BEATING HEART

A WAIT-AND-SEE-ATTITUDE was our only option as we made our way out of the last subdivision in Fort McMurray. I had been on the road for more than six hours and never left the city limits. Every direction I turned, every decision I made, was reversed by the course of the fire. The municipal Emergency Operations Centre had staggered neighbourhood evacuations in an attempt to control the number of vehicles on the road. They feared a city-wide exodus would clog streets and bring traffic to a standstill with bottlenecks trapping cars in the path of the fire. I had shuttled from neighbourhood to neighbourhood, flowing with the staggered evacuations.

Now, every soul still left in town was pouring onto already-jammed streets. With every vehicle on the road, the risk that all traffic would come to a halt and stop everyone dead in their tracks was at its height. We learned later that the Royal Canadian Air Force was on standby with transport aircraft used in remote locations like Afghanistan, able to land in the most rugged conditions. If traffic stopped moving, that was the final option.

When Steve and I made it to the exit ramp, we realized it was the last junction from which we could turn south. If we went north, it would be impossible to turn back against the tide. All lanes flowed north in an armada of mammoth Ford F-150 trucks and tiny Austin Mini Coopers, Harley-Davidson motorcycles, shiny minivans and rust-covered beaters, Winnebagos, trailered boats and all-terrain vehicles. At the time, looking at the seemingly endless convoy of bumper-to-bumper traffic disappearing into the smoke, I thought of the World War II evacuation of Dunkirk, when hundreds of British civilians launched their small ships to rescue more than 300,000 Allied troops from the bombed-out shores of France. I have always been intrigued by the idea of ordinary people confronted by a desperate situation and struggling to rise to the occasion, forced to make split-second decisions with no do-overs. It is a theme I return to time and again in my short crime stories, which are heavy on character develop-ment and snappy dialogue and light on cops-and-robber plotting. As the crime writer Dashiell Hammett once noted, I have never found the challenge to be as compelling as the behaviour of the people confronted with it. Now my life was imitating my art, with every ship a-sail, all hands on deck, the stakes life or death.

Every vehicle on the road that day contained its own story and over the next months we would hear many of them. Teachers calmed children whose parents had not been able to make it back from jobs at industry sites an hour or more north of town. Seniors' aides tried to make elderly nursing home residents comfortable on the hard-backed seats of a school bus, followed by a volunteer driver in a pickup truck ferrying wheelchairs and walkers. Cab drivers stopped at out-of-gas vehicles on the roadside to pick up passengers they would never charge. Staff from donut shops walked up and down rows of cars at a virtual stand-still to hand out coffee and baked goods hurriedly collected from the shelves as they closed shop. Families divided across multiple vehicles kept cell phone lines open in case they got separated as they merged into the endless stream of traffic. Everyone was working their way

north towards the largely First Nations and Metis hamlet of Fort McKay—almost a forty-five-minute drive in the best of conditions—and the oil sands work camps now doubling as evacuation shelters, most already full.

If Steve and I went with the flow we would keep pushing north, farther from gas pumps and supplies, from everything. If we went south, we had a chance to make it to Edmonton. CBC Radio reported that Highway 63 south might—they could not confirm—be open again. Steve phoned his communications contact in the Emergency Operations Centre to get verification. His contact had heard the same report but could not corroborate it; too much information was flowing too quickly. We knew, though, that the fire crews were desperately trying to open the road, that it was a vital route for escape and for help that might be on its way from the south.

We had three-quarters of a tank of gas and we were a dozen cars from the ramp. It was time to pick a direction.

"North, there are cars as far as I can see," I said.

"If we go south and turn back we'll still end up at the end of that line," Steve said.

"We're almost out of food and we don't have any water," I said. "They'll be running low up north."

"I'll need a high-speed Internet connection," Steve said. "There is going to be a lot of information to post online."

"How far do you think we can make it?" I said.

"It's 275 miles to Edmonton," said Steve.

"This is like that scene in the Blues Brothers movie when Elwood and Jake are deciding whether to drive all night to Chicago," I said.

"So?" said Steve.

"Hit it," I said.

We headed south.

When I remember our drive through the burning city, I think of a theme park where the most exciting roller coaster ride has the longest line. We had waited, hot, sweaty and thirsty, in a long, snaking line of

restless people. We inched forward to the front of the line. Finally, it was our turn.

I have heard that Space Mountain is one of the slower roller coasters at Disney World, with a top speed around twenty-eight miles an hour, much slower than it feels while you are moving. It's the sudden drops, loud noises and the startling images that make you feel you're flying through the stars. That was what it felt like as, strapped in our seats, we zoomed along, hearts pounding, gasping and twisting our necks as a new spectacle leapt out around every turn.

We saw no flames for the first few kilometres yet the trip felt eerie, especially with the smoky haze blanketing the road. We travelled well under the speed limit of seventy kilometres an hour. After hours at a virtual standstill, it felt like we were flying.

It also felt like we were alone. Word had not yet spread that south-bound lanes were open, so there were few cars on the highway. Ordinarily at that time of day, we would see families in vans and pickups headed to dance and judo lessons, buses with shift workers heading to and from work and truckloads of fuel and supplies heading to the industry sites.

During the boom years, traffic was nonstop bumper-to-bumper between the downtown and the newer subdivisions to the north. In addition to people heading to work and school, there were massive commercial trucks—some bigger than our house and requiring special flagged escort vehicles—shuttling back and forth to the industry sites that produced almost two per cent of Canada's gross domestic product. Morning rush hour in Fort McMurray was as congested as that of metropolitan areas like Edmonton or Calgary, or even Toronto or Vancouver. It was so dense, and the impact on the oil sands industry so costly, that the province built three side-by-side bridges to span the Athabasca River. The Alberta government gave each bridge a separate name and treated them as separate projects, claiming an overall investment of two hundred and thirty-six million dollars in the tripartite network that separated longer haul and large commercial vehicles

from local commuter traffic. The interconnected network over the Athabasca River saw five lanes going south and another five north, connecting northern subdivisions with the main highway, the downtown and the high-load bypasses.

These bridges were the first piece of critical infrastructure the Emergency Operations Centre was trying to protect. They were vulnerable to fire because intense heat inflicts structural damage on concrete and steel that can strain weight-bearing ability. Losing the bridges would break a vital transportation link, stranding evacuees in the north and cutting off supplies from the south. The only way in and out would be by air and then Fort McMurray might as well be Kabul.

The fire had not reached the bridge as Steve and I crossed it, rounding the long bend into the downtown. I looked into the river valley to see if the flames had reached the municipal water treatment plant. Surrounded by boreal forest, the plant perched across from the juncture where the Horse River emptied into the Athabasca at the foot of Abasand Hill.

I knew from my work on emergency management teams that the water treatment plant was now the most crucial building in town. It's always important, it keeps drinking water safe, as well as water for showers, laundry and dishes, all of which people take for granted when they turn on the tap. During a fire, staff workers at the plant shepherd the town's water supply, directing it to hydrants at hot spots and maintaining the right pressure for the fire hoses. That can mean low water pressure in one neighbourhood while the main flow of water is diverted to another. But this fire was everywhere.

I knew, too, that Fort McMurray's water treatment facility was only three years old and state-of-the-art, processing thirty-two million litres of water a day. I also knew the equipment hadn't been fully commissioned. When the fire was over, there would be weeks of boil water advisories, pipes to be flushed and tested, bacterial levels to monitor and adjust. But that was ahead.

We saw no sign of fire trucks around the plant but Steve and I knew—or we hoped—workers in the control room were monitoring computer screens and programming the water flow. The next day, fire crews would focus much of their efforts on the forest around the facility. The fire would scorch its walls, damaging the siding on the water intake building and destroying a storage hut. It would be that day, as exhausted fire crews threw everything they had at saving the water treatment plant, that the fire headed towards our home across the Athabasca River in a second assault on Abasand.

As we drove past, I was relieved to see there were no flames in the trees that studded the sixty-foot embankment along Abasand Hill on the end of our neighbourhood.

"I think our house is still okay," I said.

"So far, so good," said Steve.

"We might be fine," I said.

"Uh-oh," said Steve.

On the other side of the highway, on the edge of the downtown, a family home was burning and there were no fire trucks in sight. It was an ordinary ranch house, the kind seen everywhere in a downtown built by oil companies in the 1970s during their first big push into the community. We had looked at several when we were house shopping. They had extra-tall doorways and heavy wooden beams hewn from local pine, wood-burning stoves in basement rec rooms, smaller kitchens and larger yards. Many had well-kept lots where enthusiastic gardeners nurtured tomatoes and lettuce through the north's short growing season, seeding plants indoors around Easter and carefully monitoring frost levels until it was time to transplant. We had toured one ambitious garden with a dozen stalks of corn, just a few blocks from the home where flames were shooting from the roof.

"It is possible," I said. For the first time that day my hands shook. "The downtown could burn."

"It looks like it," said Steve.

How the home caught fire, given it was across four lanes of concrete highway and well away from the burning boreal forest, was likely related to a rare weather pattern. Around 10:30 AM, as I was unpacking groceries, there had been what meteorologists call an inversion—a dramatic, instant change in atmospheric conditions as a cap of cold air trapped warmer air near the ground. This was dangerous because of a trio of climatic conditions that were extremely rare in a Fort McMurray spring: very high temperatures, very low relative humidity and extremely strong winds. Even more grave, there had been no rain for weeks, little winter snow, and virtually no spring snow pack—turning the woods into kindling. The inversion was like pouring gasoline on tinder, creating the perfect conditions for an explosive surge when a reckless ATV rider carelessly sparked a fire in the woods.

On the previous Sunday afternoon, when Steve and I first saw the plume of smoke from the Abasand trail, the fire was two hectares in size. By 6:00 PM—two hours later—it had raced through the dry forest bed and ballooned to sixty hectares. Now, two days later, as we drove down Highway 63, it stretched for thousands of hectares, the heat so intense it created its own lightning. This set of meteorological conditions meant a blizzard of embers was carried on the high winds to randomly drift down on dry grass, leaves, pine needles, fences, patio decks, wood piles and rooftops like the one burning in the downtown.

The fire's rapacious hunger made it seem surreal, prompting descriptions of it as living thing, a monster bent on destruction, a supernatural entity with evil intent. The image seemed borne out by movie-like scenes where, just as firefighters gained the upper hand, flames roared back to life stronger than before. I never bought into that image. It was a forest fire caused by a careless idiot who dropped a cigarette or sparked an engine in an area with a well-publicized burn ban. A human being did something treacherously, colossally rash. The fire wasn't supernatural. It was caused by stupidity and criminal negligence. Later, when I had to describe it, I called it the Horse River

Wildfire. I gave an angry, vicious and obscene title to the anonymous person who started the fire, something I would be embarrassed to see in print.

At the next intersection, another three hundred metres past the burning house, we saw the next piece of critical infrastructure, the Northern Lights Regional Health Centre, the only hospital in town. When I had driven out of Abasand, it was a scene of intense activity, crowded with vehicles and people, stretchers and wheelchairs and ambulances and buses. At one point, a helicopter landed in the hospital parking lot to airlift a critically-ill patient. Now that parking lot was deserted. The patients, medical charts, and medications had been packed onto seventeen buses headed north to an oil sands site with its own airstrip. From there they flew to Edmonton, fanned out to a host of hospitals and continuing care centres. In less than two hours, the staff evacuated 109 patients, including nine babies in the neonatal unit.

Fort McMurray is proud of its high birth rate, boasting 147 babies born in one month in the summer of 2012. The day of the fire, in addition to newborns whose first hours of life were spent fleeing the city of their birth, there were hundreds of babies, hundreds of pregnant women, and thousands of children sharing the road. Later, a provincial health study would look at the evacuation's impact on expectant mothers and babies born after the fire. Nine months after the fire, in a typical McMurray donnybrook, there would be a feisty debate over what constituted a "fire baby" as hundreds of McMurray women became pregnant in the days and weeks after the fire. As the high birth rate continues, so does the importance of the hospital. A major capital fundraising campaign had brought in more than half a million dollars at the annual holiday fundraiser six months before the fire. Steve and I hoped that this money would not be needed to rebuild a facility destroyed by fire, but it was going to be close. Earlier that day firefighters had stood on the hospital roof and hosed it down.

Just a few hundred metres away, on the other side of the highway, the pine trees on the southern slope of Abasand Hill flared like too

many candles jammed onto a birthday cake. A fresh, jagged scar had been cut down the middle of the burning hill where a heroic driver in a large white truck had smashed through a gate and led an exodus of family vehicles down what had been a footpath. Now there were no vehicles, not even fire trucks, in sight.

At the foot of the burning hill, in a valley on the banks of the Hangingstone River, was the small neighbourhood of Grayling Terrace. An exclusive area, it was home to middle-class professionals, engineers, reclamation experts, teachers, nurses, and people who coached youth hockey, brought snacks to soccer games, and gave to the United Way. Built on a flood plain, it had been evacuated in 2013 as the Hangingstone River overflowed. I had visited the site with the emergency team to deal with a young reporter who slipped past a safety barricade and into the danger zone. At the time, the flood destruction seemed widespread, the bulldozers and sandbags along the river banks an all-hands-on-deck operation. Now we saw two houses on fire, jarringly closer to the highway than the flaming trees. Just across the Hangingstone River, Beacon Hill's northern ridge was engulfed in flame.

Also built mostly during the 1970s, the Beacon Hill neighbourhood was, as the name suggests, atop a hill. It attracted longer-term community residents, many of them administrative staff in the government and non-profit institutions centred in the downtown. It was also home to blue-collar workers in the nearby industrial Gregoire, one of the first neighbourhoods to be evacuated. Out-of-town media had started the day in Gregoire, escorted by fire and municipal officials, and we'd heard reports about Beacon Hill and Gregoire throughout the day. Now we saw it for ourselves, the burnt-out shells of a trailer park, motel and a gas station, flames licking the ditches on both sides of the highway.

During the 2013 flood, Beacon Hill, on some of the highest ground in town, was outside the danger zone and its Frank Lacroix Arena had served as the main evacuation centre. The arena was a throwback

compared with the town's newer recreational facilities, gleaming multi-storey glass and steel structures named for corporations instead of people like Lacroix, a volunteer hockey coach. Lacroix arena is a typical Canadian hockey "barn" with wooden boards surrounding an NHL-sized ice surface. During the flood, the ice surface was given over to one hundred cots for evacuees. At the time it seemed a massive mobilization of resources, although the shelter was almost empty when I had arrived there with the mayor and fire chief. McMurray residents had opened their doors to evacuees, offering home-cooked meals and comfortable mattresses. Fewer than a dozen people opted for the cots: independent types who saw the evacuation shelter as an overnight way station before returning to their homes in the neighbourhood of Waterways.

Waterways was McMurray's oldest and quirkiest neighbourhood, with the highest percentage of residents who boasted—and they loved to boast—of being born in town. Vocal and engaged, they held pivotal power in local elections, knew their own minds, were fiercely independent and often downright cranky. Mobile home owners there resisted evacuating even as their units were in danger of being swept away by flood waters. It would not have surprised me to see a Waterways trailer home floating down the cresting Clearwater River with a pirate flag hoisted over the bow.

Waterways was a jigsaw puzzle of buildings that started along the Clearwater and ambled back towards the highway, most under two storeys, a hodgepodge of wooden houses and sheds and garages, industrial buildings cheek to jowl with family homes. It had sprung up in the 1920s when it was the end of the line for the Alberta and Great Waterways Railway, the northernmost point on the North American railroad grid. Cargo headed further north was unloaded from boxcars and transferred to barges where fleets of tugboats ferried it north on the Mackenzie River watershed and into the Northwest Territories and the Yukon.

Almost a century later, Waterways had embraced the oil boom in its own unique fashion. A sleek late-model luxury car could be parked next to a twenty-five-year-old rust bucket. Jeans and plaid shirts were the standard uniform, making it impossible to tell if you were talking to someone down on their luck or a millionaire who cashed in on the property boom. It was home to the local Royal Canadian Legion, and the gateway to a past of fur traders and lone Mounties. It was also the subject of an A.Y. Jackson painting that hangs in the National Gallery of Canada, the image of a giant tipi overshadowing a tiny church. The artist's original small study of the work had hung outside my door at my college job, and I loved it for its power and vibrancy. Waterways was the beating heart of a quirky, cranky, nutty town that weathered boom and bust. As Steve and I drove past, every inch of it seemed on fire.

I could feel my heart pounding. My open mouth gasped for breath in the smoky air inside the car. I was thirsty and nauseated but there was nowhere to pull over to be sick. My shoulders hunched and I looked at my feet in the sneakers I put on to run down the stairs of my house. It seemed hotter, although for the first time that day we were driving away from the flames.

Then, in another twist of the bizarre weather patterns assaulting the city, we emerged from the smoke to see blue sky and blazing sun, the same beautiful day I had driven through earlier on my way to the grocery store. Just ahead, a lone police officer waved frantically, urging us to head south in the northbound lanes of the only highway out of town.

7 | THE BIBLE AND THE BEE BOOK

THEY CALL IT THE HIGHWAY OF DEATH. Suicide 63. Hell's Highway. There was a popular Canadian television show about the life-threatening work of pulling spectacular wrecks from the snowy banks of Highway 63. It was a reality program that was all too real.

Highway 63 is the main road, the only road, to and from the oil sands of northeastern Alberta. At any time of day or night the long, isolated stretch of asphalt, lined with trees and snow and not much else, is packed with traffic, much of it enormous transport trucks with super-wide, oversized loads. The trucks crawl down the road like cranky snapping turtles, slow, heavy, determined and dangerous if surprised.

The highway also carries every person in Fort McMurray who wants to buy bunk beds for their kids or service a foreign car or buy bulk steel-cut oats at Costco in Edmonton. Drivers who might have worked a double shift with no sleep. Drivers stuck behind a wide load for hours, finally deking around it at top speed to make up for lost time.

The oil companies stress safe driving. Some believe that's because they are obsessed with lost hours and the bottom line, and some that it's genuine concern for workers. It's probably both. Oil company

vehicles are carefully and clearly marked for optimal visibility with bright orange flags on long sticks—buggy whips they are called in the trade—popping jauntily from the beds of pickup trucks, "pilot" vehicles that guide mammoth trucks, some with tires one storey high and a ladder to climb into the driver's cab.

The orange flags fascinate journalists from major American centres like New York or Washington or Los Angeles, who first arrived to write about the oil boom, then the bust, and then the fire recovery. Male American reporters—never, for some reason, Canadian ones—insist on going to the town's one strip club and interviewing the customers. (Apparently, there are no strip clubs in New York City. Who knew?) They almost never go to one of the many well-tended high school sports fields and talk to the student athletes, some of whom play on better turf than Canadian Football League players.

One of the reasons American reporters head to the strip club, aside from the obvious, is to find people who aren't at work. Everyone who comes to McMurray—and they come from everywhere: Newfoundland, Somalia, Spain, India, America, The Philippines, Pakistan, Bolivia—comes to work. Engineers, accountants, nurses, teachers, baristas, chefs and bus drivers. The rhythm of McMurray is that of shifts—fourteen days on and seven off, seven on and seven off, six on and one off. It is not unusual for a shift to last twelve hours. Workers have been known to play out shifts between two or three different companies, thinking that if they have come to McMurray to work, they will work all hours. It continues since the layoffs of the economic downturn, with fewer people working longer and more frequent shifts, making for a lot of tired people in a hurry.

So, even with the training and the buggy whips, and ambitious road construction by the provincial government, Highway 63 maintains its reputation. From 2008 to 2012, it saw 130 head-on collisions; many because an impatient driver pulled out to pass a vehicle and crashed into oncoming traffic at full speed. In 2012, the year Steve and I arrived, the community was in mourning after a devastating crash

on a snowy night killed seven people. Over the past fifteen years, the total death toll on the highway approaches one hundred people. There are parents in southern Alberta who still won't allow their children's sports teams to play tournaments in McMurray because they won't risk their families' lives on the Highway of Death.

Highway of Death. Suicide 63. Hell's Highway.

It sounds melodramatic, but that's what I thought when the lone Royal Canadian Mounted Police officer at the intersection waved agitatedly through the smoke to send Steve and me and our little blue car speeding southbound on the northbound lanes of Highway 63.

As we approached the intersection, I put down my cell phone and put my hand on Steve's arm. I wanted to take his hand but he was clutching the steering wheel and unconsciously leaning forward, as if urging us forward.

"Here we go," said Steve, as we flew past the young man in a blue uniform and black boots, no hat, legs apart, alone in the middle of the road. His cruiser was parked a few yards behind him with lights flashing. He was probably, like many RCMP officers in the community, a recruit fresh from "Depot Division," the cadet academy. He wore a small white mask over his nose and mouth. The mask looked useless. I don't know where he was supposed to go if the fire turned towards him. I doubt anyone gave him instructions for that worst-case scenario. It was one of the bravest stands I have ever seen. I tried not to think of other drivers headed in his direction; some might be panicked, might have been awake for twenty-four hours, might even have been having a drink when the call came in to get out of town.

That day, all over that city, young men and women stood in the path of the fire, some alone and some in teams, like the young men and women in uniform I saw guiding the pumper truck up Abasand Hill in a faint hope gesture, racing into a neighbourhood past saving. But they never once looked back.

There is so much you hear about Fort McMurray. Deeply disturbing issues surrounding fossil fuels are laid at its door. Time and again,

celebrities fly in on private airplanes to attack the community that extracted the materials for their jet fuel.

Like everyone in Fort McMurray, and I mean everyone, I have complicated feelings about oil extraction. People in McMurray recycle and conserve electricity and think about their carbon footprint. We worry about the environment and our families and the future. We wonder if we are more complicit if we work in extraction than those who use the products of that extraction. We are aware—and since the fire a lot more Canadian are aware—what happens to the country's gross domestic product if the oil sands shut down and the federal and provincial tax revenue slows.

The residents of McMurray are aware of what is made from oil and what is not. We understand changes are coming, that changes must come, and educate ourselves about the future. We think about it, and talk about it, every day.

For the rest of my life, the first image of McMurray that will spring to my mind is of a young RCMP constable alone in the middle of an intersection while flames creep along the side of the highway and cars full of desperate families speed past. I have never been so frightened as when we sped past him going more than one hundred kilometres an hour southbound in the northbound lane of Suicide 63.

"I bet a lot of people are praying for us," I said.

"Pretty safe bet," said Steve.

"I saved Saint Therese," I said. "She's in the back. I didn't pack her very well. She might be smashed."

"Maybe not," said Steve.

"I saved your family Bible, too," I said.

"Then we're covered," said Steve. "Good to know."

"I also took your bee book."

"What more do we need?" said Steve.

The books had been in Steve's family for generations. The Bible lists every family birth and death, Roy's passing recently written into the pages by Steve's sister. It is a worn, well-thumbed King James

Version with a faded black leather cover soft from handling. Roy always claimed his lifelong interest in things spiritual began with that Bible, which he read cover to cover one winter the family was snowed in on their farm. He could quote passages he felt appropriate to an occasion, although he was prone to pop out bits he thought funny, like "my brother is an hairy man and I am a smooth man." He liked to draw out *smoooooth* so that it sounded like a line from a skit and laugh himself silly.

Sitting on top of the family Bible was Roy's copy of *Pioneer Life On The Bay of Quinte*. The Bonisteels had come to Canada during the American Revolution as United Empire Loyalists, American colonists loyal to the Crown, and many settled in the Quinte area in Ontario. The book is a first edition from 1904 and Steve's family is one of the 309 profiled. It includes a biographical sketch about an ancestor who hid someone in a stove to escape American soldiers. The Bonisteels love that story, but I always pictured Hansel and Gretel and the witch. I had taken the book, though.

Stacked on top of *Pioneer Life* was a book about beekeeping that belonged to Steve's grandfather, Benson Bonisteel. Written in the late nineteenth century by A.I Root and E.R. Root—perfect names for agricultural writers—it was called *The ABC And XYZ Of Bee Culture*. It remains, so Steve tells me, the beekeeper's bible. Little in the life of a bee, I understand, has changed since it was written, and colonies, feeding and building hives are constants. Steve's edition is from the 1920s, well-used and well-kept. Folded carefully among its pages was Benson's Province of Ontario beekeeping licence, almost a mirror of one Steve applied for two generations later. He kept hives as a boy and hopes with a nerdish fervour to keep them again someday.

I listed other items I had packed, in no particular order, and Steve praised me for every little effort. I praised him for filling up the gas tank and remembering his leftover lunch so I had something to eat. We opened one of the drinks I tossed in the car. We composed texts and emails to our families. Steve kept driving, I kept typing, and

messages kept coming in, growing more frantic as the news coverage of the fire intensified.

My sister-in-law Mandy is a woman of action, a problem solver and a bottomless fount of kindness. If we asked her to rent a Winnebago in Toronto and meet us in Edmonton, she would have been halfway to Regina by dawn. She was, of course, one of the first people asking how she could help.

"What should I tell her?" I asked.

"Tell her we have the bee book," Steve said.

'We have the bee book,' I typed.

'What?' Mandy typed back.

"Tell her the bee book is safe," Steve said.

'The bee book is safe,' I typed. I got another instant reply.

"She wants to know what we need," I said.

Steve paused. "Bees."

Now that Steve and I have been married more than two decades, people sometimes ask me why some marriages last. Is it shared values or space for growth? Fresh experiences or common history? Yada-yada-yada. I have no idea. I do have one suggestion for a couple thinking about a lifetime commitment. You should find the same things funny.

That night on the Highway of Death, we laughed so hard at Steve's bad bee joke I am surprised that we didn't drive off the road and cause the night's only major collision. We were still giddy when, a few hours later, we reached Wandering River, the first major stop south of Fort McMurray. Somehow, we still had a quarter tank of gas as we pulled into the line for the fuel pumps. It was close to dusk and the line of cars was excruciatingly long, more than one hundred cars, circling out of the parking lot and down the road.

We wondered if the station—or our car—would run out of gas before we made it to the pump. We had no idea how much fuel was stored there. We heard on CBC Radio that people in Edmonton were filling up containers of gasoline and heading north to help fire refugees

stranded on the side of the road. We decided to roll the dice and head for Grasslands, the next major stop on the Highway of Death. If we ran out of gas, we would spend the night in the car, well away from the fire, and hope for the kindness of strangers. We hit the road again, without coffee and out of snacks, determined to keep each other awake.

"How about some music?" Steve said.

We didn't have any of the hundreds of compact discs we started collecting when we first met, when I pioneered a live music column at the local newspaper. The column was popular, Kingston's music scene influenced by the success of The Tragically Hip. Our CD collection started with The Hip and Kingston bands like The Headstones and The Mahones, and grew with singer-songwriters, the genre a special favourite for two people who made their living with words. It was our custom to travel with music—but it was so cold during Fort McMurray winters that we left nothing in our car. So, we had none of our music. We had my blasted phone. A few days before I had tried to download an album but I never got around to testing it. We needed something for the road so I decided to give it a try.

"I have no idea if I did this right," I said.

"Let's see what happens," Steve said.

The song pounded out from the tiny speaker on my phone and we almost had to pull over because we were laughing so hard. We sailed out of Wandering River, other headlights blinking on around us, listening to Warren Zevon sing, "I Was In the House When the House Burned Down."

8 | THE CAT PHOTO

IT WAS 4:00 AM when we finally arrived in Edmonton—twelve hours since leaving City Hall—and somehow, on the very last leg of our journey, we made our first wrong turn. We missed the off-ramp and drove away from the hotel a friend booked for us while we drove. Now the little blue dot on the online map was moving in the opposite direction. We were tired and thirsty, sweaty without air conditioning, choked with smoke and ash and hoarse from talking to stay awake. I kept my eyes clapped on the little blue dot and willed it across the finish line.

I have never felt so relieved as when we finally tumbled though the door of an ordinary beige room in a business-travel hotel near the West Edmonton Mall. It was the end of a journey that started with me alone and scrambling madly in our home, making split-second decisions about what to take and tossing the items into a small blue box. After a too-long evacuation of our neighbourhood, stop-and-go in a lineup on the only road, watching ash waft down to coat the windshield, I had made it to Steve's workplace. Then the two of us travelled for hours in thirty-four-degree Celsius heat, me answering emails and text messages

from frightened family members while Steve drove past flames and through clouds of smoke. Then there we were, in a clean, well-lit hotel room.

We had no night clothes or toiletries when we arrived, not even a toothbrush. In the rush to leave, I hadn't thought to pack the ordinary items that I'd normally take on a trip. Our clothes were soaked with smoke but we weren't aware of the woodsy musk until we walked into a spotless hotel room. We showered and slid between the crisp, clean sheets, falling instantly asleep.

When we awoke, we had a lingering worry that everyone had not made it out of the chaos alive, that there was much we didn't know. We tried to be cautiously optimistic. But if we got up we would turn on the television to watch the morning news, which was something we usually did when travelling. When we turned on the news we would see more images of an inferno and long lines of slow-moving cars. We would see the same on the front page of the newspaper on the stand in the hallway by the elevators. But we couldn't just lie there.

"Let's get up," I said.

"Good idea," said Steve.

"If we get up now and then go to bed early we can get back on a regular schedule," I said. "Like we just flew to Europe and we're adjusting to the local time zone."

"Good idea," said Steve. "Let's do it."

But we didn't. We lay on our backs and held hands in the king-sized bed, curtains closed, not checking phones or emails. We talked about how lucky we were, how well our little car had done, how one tank of gas had lasted so long, how well Steve had driven, how well I had packed the Go Bag, how wonderful our friend Ashley had been to book us this hotel, how soft the bed was, how the breakfast that started in an hour sounded nice. We were in fine shape.

We decided to answer the most urgent phone calls then head down to the lobby for breakfast. We would power through the day and then we would head home in a day or two.

We stayed there for ten days.

The first morning was busy. The hotel breakfast bar filled up as people made their way to the lobby in yoga pants and pajama bottoms, and socks instead of slippers. It felt like a huge extended family bunking together over the holidays, foraging in a half-familiar kitchen to mix the nourishing with the treats.

Throughout the morning, the same conversation looped over and over as friends and family met up or answered constantly ringing cell phones. I heard people—I heard myself—start the story with how beautiful the previous day had been, how the smoke had been heading away from town, and how we were doing everyday chores, such as grocery shopping and laundry, before the wind shifted.

People joked about the things they took and the things they didn't think to take, passports, underwear and phone chargers. Every time a new group of evacuees arrived, they told the same story—with the same words.

"We were lucky. We gassed up the car the night before."

"I just noticed my shoes don't match."

"We were lucky. I had all my credit cards in my purse."

"I don't have to worry about planting those shrubs."

"We were lucky. A lot of people have it worse."

We were all in shock, dazed, numb and in denial. But the mood was upbeat that day and long afterwards, at least in the public areas of the hotel. Surprisingly, the mood was just as cheery among the long lines of exhausted shoppers flocking to nearby stores looking for the essentials they had forgotten to pack in the hasty evacuation. A west Edmonton Walmart—one of the few stores that didn't offer discounts to evacuees—completely sold out of men's underwear and pajamas. But most stores were offering discounts and waved away proof of evacuation. I asked one clerk if that helped to keep the lines moving. He told me one look was enough to tell if the red-eyed, rumpled customer with the large stack of socks and T-shirts had fled the fire.

The hotel was full of babies, toddlers and preschoolers, which only added to the feeling that we were part of a large, extended family. A little girl with a peanut butter sandwich cut into squares balanced it carefully in one hand as she played concierge and pushed the elevator button for us. The lobby was filled with small boys in superhero pajamas and girls wearing butterfly wings. They skipped up and down the halls, bouncing in excitement at the waffle machine and the endless supply of chocolate milk, leaving puddles in the hallway after splashing down the pool's water slide. Pizza deliveries came and went, books were read on the lobby couch, people waited for relatives, for the Red Cross, for news that the fire had been brought under control.

Most people had no idea if their homes were still standing. The devastation was too large; there was no master list of what was lost. There was also a randomness to the fire's pattern. It razed some properties and swerved around others. Homes directly in the fire's path were somehow spared, while other properties thought to be safe went up in flames. Some homes had to be bulldozed by desperate officials constructing firebreaks to save a larger neighbourhood. We suspected our home was gone but couldn't be certain. All resources were directed to fighting the fire, which continued to grow. The tally of damage would come later.

As the week wore on, the hotel grew busier, partly because it was offering a deep discount to evacuees. No one knew when the evacuation would end. The lobby was full at every hour of the day as northern evacuation camps emptied out and convoys of families were escorted through the burnt-out city and south down Highway 63. The reception desk was fully staffed at all hours, cleaning crews working nonstop to turn over rooms, check ins and check outs were constant as people came and went, eventually arranging to stay with family and friends in nearby towns. Steve and I, with most of our family in eastern Canada, stayed put. The staff at the hotel worked steadily, never enforcing breakfast hours, letting bleary-eyed parents come and go, refilling juice

bars, stacking newspapers, pouring out waffle mix and wiping up puddles from the swimming pool.

I watched science fiction movies, texted photos of Saint Therese to family and friends. I went shopping because Steve, his feet blistered from the dress shoes he had been wearing the day of the fire, needed slippers to wear in the hotel room while he sat at the narrow desk. While Steve worked sixteen hours a day and more at his computer, I called our insurance company and filled prescriptions. I bought two ceramic mugs with silly cat faces because we kept spilling from the paper cups from the in-room coffee machine. We ate excellent meals featuring bison meatballs, elk lasagna and bannock and maple butter at the on-site restaurant ironically named Homefire.

It was at that restaurant that I cried for the first time. We'd finished another fine dinner when the waitress told us a regular customer had anonymously paid our bill after overhearing us talking about the evacuation. After days of coping, I was a puddle of tears.

People have told me over and over since then how a small act of kindness triggered a similar waterfall of tears. A mother cried over her son's free bag of Legos. A firefighter teared up when thanked for his service. People wept over sharing homemade sandwiches, at waived fees, refunded tickets and free cab rides.

"I don't know why I'm crying," I said. "A lot of people have it worse."

"They do," said Steve, reaching across the table to hold my hand.

"We were lucky," I said.

"We are," he said.

The first Saturday after the fire, Steve finally took a few hours off from work, no texting, phone calls or emails. We sat on the bed and watched, as we had for years, the annual Kentucky Derby. We ate microwaved popcorn in pop-up bowls and drank cherry cola. I can't remember which horse won. After the race, Steve sat down at his computer and started work again.

Every day, while Steve hunched over the little desk across from the bed, I tried to stay busy. The first few days had been taken up with

phone calls and emails assuring family and friends we were safe. People urged me to look after myself and I took it to heart, exercising in the hotel gym, buying vitamins, drinking lots of water. I am allergic to lanolin, often found in hotel soaps and shampoos, so I went out for toiletries that would not make me break out in an angry red rash. I shopped for T-shirts, for sweatpants, for pajamas, for socks. I bought a water bottle. Every day I went to a store and bought a few more items, only to realize the next day that I needed something else. I bought paper plates and plastic cutlery so that we would not have to eat every meal out. I found myself saying, "The last thing I need is another coffee mug." Then I realized, "'Oh, wait a minute. I might have no coffee mugs at all."

Soon I stopped reading the free hotel newspaper, the front pages filled with stories and photographs from the fire. I stopped watching the television news. I watched an entire season of a show about a Zombie detective. I went to a local bookstore and bought a collection of works by Dashiell Hammett, whom I adore because he writes my kind of stories, long on quirky characters and snappy dialogue, with wobbly cops-and-robbers-plots. I annoyed Steve by reading some of my favourite lines out to him while he tried to work.

"I don't mind a reasonable amount of trouble," I read. I snorted and a little of the water I was drinking came out my nose. "That's my new motto."

"I thought your motto was 'You got to look on the bright side, even if there ain't one'," said Steve.

"That's my old motto," I said.

"I have to work," said Steve.

"I know," I said.

I spent too much time looking out the window at the vacant lot behind the hotel and watched evacuees walk their dogs. I counted the breeds, from teacup terriers to an almost-full-grown Newfoundland dog. Most had no leashes. A few chased balls or squeaky plastic bones but most did not because their owners had not remembered to bring dog toys as they fled.

As the week stretched on it became apparent that many evacuees had to leave pets behind. On the morning of the fire, most people set out for work as usual, leaving only enough kibble and water for a single day. Other animals were turned loose because they couldn't fit in the family vehicle but might have a chance at outrunning the flames. Stories began appearing in the press about animal escapes. A girl had ridden her horse down the highway. A pot-bellied pig was coaxed to shelter by a firefighter offering a piece of watermelon. A gerbil got a book deal and a visit with the premier of Alberta. Donations of pet food came in from across Canada.

Steve's online duties that week included creating the municipality's pet rescue web application, allowing people to report a pet left behind in Fort McMurray, relaying information to the bylaw officers who, bonded and screened, could legally enter a home and take the animal to a shelter. From my point of view, Steve's application was also a work of art. The code he crafted, labouring over each line until it was exactly right, reached out to evacuees and gave them a voice. I saw this in his decision to create a method for people to post a photograph of their left-behind pet, partly a safety feature to let bylaw officers know whether Fluffy was a Yorkshire terrier or a Rottweiler, but also much more meaningful. There were more than 600 requests to the pet rescue site by end of the first week, almost all with a photograph. Most evacuees had their cell phones and so most had photographs of their pet, snapshots of domestic life before it was brutally disrupted. Two tabby cats curled together in a chair, a snow-white rabbit hopped around a classroom of laughing children, a neatly groomed dog pranced in his backyard. Fish, iguanas, hamsters, even a flock of homing pigeons, were the living, breathing symbols of homes abandoned in the path of the fire. I, too, felt the powerful connection between a pet and a sense of belonging. One of the tokens I took as I headed out was a photograph of my favourite cat.

Cats showed up frequently in the pages of my family's photo albums. Every few years we chose a kitten from a litter at someone's

farm and brought it home, where it remained an "outdoor" cat because there were no litter boxes in my mother's tidy house. They were mousers, expected to earn their keep like everyone in our family (except my father).

One cat appears often in our childhood photographs, a ginger tom that went fishing with my sisters and me. For us, fishing was an all-day affair, starting with the bait. We used plastic beach shovels to carefully dig in our mother's perfect garden for fat brown dew worms, dirt clinging to their sticky sides as they wiggled in the unexpected sunlight. We plopped the worms into a plastic bucket filled with warm earth. The cat got excited when it saw us pick up a plastic shovel. It would watch us dig and then march behind us as we carried the bucket down the hill that started with our front lawn, across a road that saw little traffic, and down a rutted path to the shoreline where Lake Ontario met the St. Lawrence River.

We could not afford new poles, so the four of us shared two broken bass rods from the fishing camp where our father sometimes worked as a guide. Our father gave us basic instructions: use small hooks (which were all we had anyway) keep the line a foot off the bottom, and pull up when the red-and-white bobber dipped. The busted reels didn't turn, so we'd lift the rods high in the air to pull out the line, sometimes hauling it in with our bare hands. He also gave us one of the few pieces of advice he ever shared: "Fish don't bite in an on-shore wind."

We were after the quick-moving perch, which we and the cat could see darting around in the water. We caught sunfish with bright yellow bellies and green-grey rock bass, bony and not worth cleaning, but the cat found them delicious and we always fed him one. There were lots of photos of my sisters and I sitting on the dock holding up a fish, the cat staring at our catch.

The only pet photo I have now is of a different cat, an orange-and-white tom. That photo sat on my desk in the same spot where the cat had once perched, watching me write. I picked him out as a kitten at the shelter and named him Hank Williams. Hank was the first

commitment of my life away from the Island after my father died.
I dragged him from pillar to post, from the undergraduate university
I attended on an academic scholarship, to my graduate scholarship at
another university, to my first newspaper job back in Kingston, travel-
ling with an old car, a few books, some clothes, the cat and his food bowl.

When Steve and I moved in together, he and the cat fought a
running battle. Every night, Hank would settle at the bottom of our
too-small double bed, a glowing mahogany Depression-era sleigh
bed that had been in Steve's grandparents' home and which weighed
hundreds of pounds. Every night Hank sprawled at the bottom and by
morning he had crept up between the two of us so Steve would wake
with the cat's ass in his face. In another trick, Hank pissed on Steve's
favourite red wool sweater, bought on our honeymoon. He managed it
so Steve wouldn't notice until he was at work and his body heat blos-
somed the unmistakable smell of cat urine.

Steve was Hank's favourite—but not his only—target. He growled
tiger-like at the adorable neighbour girls who wore pink tutus as they
rode tricycles in our driveway. He slapped my four-year-old nephew in
the face then jumped out a window. He tried to steal a steak from the
neighbour's barbecue. He killed squirrels and left their tails in the yard
like totems. He yowled for three days straight when my friend Tim,
whose photo also graced my desk, kept him while I was out of town.

In eighteen years, Hank never needed a pill or had a vet bill other
than the usual shots. When he died, stretched out comfortably under
our bedroom fan, it was his final victory against Steve. While I was still
at work, Steve scooped the cat's body into a carrier and race-walked to
the vet, passing a group of school children who wanted to look at the
kitty, forcing Steve into a run.

I had years of photographs of Hank. My favourite was a glossy
black-and-white I took, the print developed by a photojournalism
student while I was teaching college. Hank sat on a chair in our old
kitchen in Kingston, fur gleaming, gazing regally into the camera.
I kept the photo on a stairway ledge in Fort McMurray, where I saw

it every day. I thought of it as I was rushing about the house but didn't get to it. I only had time to snatch up a little snapshot I kept on my writing desk where I sat when Steve called about the evacuation.

I often dream of Hank and my dreams look like that snapshot. I hear the house keys jingling in my hand, the sound that brought Hank running when I came home. He appears at my feet, standing in a patch of bright green grass by my back door and glares up at me. I reach down to stroke him and his fur is warm and silky. His extra-long, luxurious tail, which you cannot see in the photo, is straight up in the air as he prances away inviting me to follow him. He leads me towards a lush forest, trotting ahead, sure of where he is going and that I will follow, that we are heading somewhere safe, where we are meant to be. He pads into the trees and I start to move forward.

9 | THE BREDA
NEEDLEPOINT

WHILE WE STAYED AT THE HOTEL my sleep was restless and filled with exhausting dreams. I was still in the house, racing from room to room and tossing keepsakes in the blue box, going back to get objects I had not remembered at the time. A string of images unspooled like eight-millimetre film pouring from a projector. I saw family photographs, a book report my youngest niece wrote about one of my anthologies, framed watercolour illustrations from a series of my short stories.

I saw wedding gifts. The wooden serving set we used every Christmas Eve. The hand-quilted picture of a family farm from my late Aunt Annie. The linen tablecloth and napkins from the old friend who had performed our marriage ceremony. A breadbox shaped like a London bus from another friend who had gone off to study at Oxford. The hunter green placemats my Aunt Rika sewed with scenes of the racing horses I loved as a little girl, left behind on the table made entirely from wood cut and milled on Steve's family farm.

There were gifts from people I had known forever, a ceramic Mickey Mouse Dow Ale mug from my dearest friend from university, who also gave me a three-volume set of Ontario history books,

Boswell's *Life of Johnson*, stacks of Tom Waits records, and the best dictionary I ever owned. There was a cache of the witty observational letters he sent over twenty-five years, his distinctive scrawl on pages and pages of lined yellow notepaper, funny and full of eccentric characters, quirky stories told in his wry, idiosyncratic voice. Someday, I thought, his letters would make a good book.

One morning I woke from a dream to the ringing of my cell phone and answered a call from my mother. At the sound of her voice I burst into tears. I cried into the phone as Steve squeezed my hand.

"It looked scary," my mother said. "It was on every channel. We watched it all night."

"It wasn't so bad," I said. "It looked worse on TV."

"It looked pretty bad," she said.

"There was only one time when I thought I might have to run for the river," I told her. "And it was only for a few minutes. But I could have made it easily, it was pretty close."

"I'm sure you could," she said.

My mother, who possesses the passion for organization our family considers "Dutch," asked about our next steps. I told her that we, like all evacuees, had to register with the Red Cross.

"The Red Cross," she said. "Your Grandmother Vanstrien hated them."

"Oh, right," I said. "I remember that."

"Your grandmother said the Red Cross only helped the high-class people in the town," said my mother. "If you were somebody important you got help. She said the farmers got nothing."

This was exactly the sort of thing my grandmother would have said. She said it about the electric company all the time. Also, the Conservative Party of Canada. And Protestants.

"Her whole life," my mother said, "she hated the Red Cross."

That my grandmother Petronella Rozenberg Vanstrien, my mother's mother, hated an international aid organization was not surprising. She was a Class A hater, the epitome of the modern catch

phrase "haters gonna hate"—although she would have hated the expression.

The list of things she hated was long and both general and specific. Many of the items began with the Nazi occupation of Breda, her home town in the south of the Netherlands, then a largely poor and Catholic dairy farming area near the Belgian border where my mother was born in the middle of the Second World War. My mother has no memories of the War, just bits and pieces of stories she picked up from her nine older brothers and sisters. Given that no one in the family liked to speak about it, and that every story they told turned into a domestic farce, facts were scarce. The only time my sisters and I heard anything about it was in connection with something that had made Grandma Vanstrien's hate list.

The list included: Germans (not just Nazis), Russians (both Red and White as she called them based on her own definitions and which did not mean Communists and Imperialists), Americans (took too long to get into the War, *godverdomme!*), the electric company (rip-off artists who only cared about money), farmers who left dirty, or even worse, broken (*kaput!*) farm machinery parked around the barnyard (pigs with no pride) and my father (lazy, which was true).

That my sisters and I knew what she hated, that she communicated it so clearly, was a triumph of her will because, despite living more than forty years in Canada, she never felt the need to learn English. And even though, after first setting foot on Canadian soil, at her insistence the entire Vanstrien family declared themselves Canadians, no longer Dutch. They would eat Canadian food—including sandwiches made from white Wonder Bread thickly spread with butter and sprinkled with white sugar, which I saw lots of Dutch Canadians eat but no one from my father's family, which had been in Canada since the mid-1600s. They played Canadian card games like euchre with a "kill-as-you-go" panache, in later years calling Steve a jackass every time he forgot trump. They danced like they thought Canadians danced, which meant doing the polka to country music. They were loud and

unpolished and hardworking and tireless. Within ten years of coming to Canada, most of them owned their own dairy farms.

I'm sure they knew that long-time Canadians like my father's family thought of them as "foreigners" and viewed them with suspicion for their easy independence, their liberal outlook, and even the strict work ethic and devotion to domestic cleanliness that made other homes seem dowdy and rundown by comparison. But my mother's family developed an insouciant disregard for facts they found unpleasant. If anyone dared to point out an obvious contradiction they would draw back in indignant scorn and affect the one Canadian behaviour they fully understood: Never Let On.

For people who never shut up, who never seemed to have a single unexpressed thought ("Yes, you look fat in the dress") and who said everything at the top of their lungs, they could be remarkably reticent. Among the many subjects of which they never spoke, most had to do with the War and the period just before the liberation when my grandfather, Johannes Cornelius Vanstrien, was imprisoned. They had no trouble speaking about my grandfather in general. They could talk for hours of his death a few years after immigrating to Canada, in the sunshine one fine summer day on the farm he no longer rented but owned outright, dropping dead from a heart attack while plowing a hayfield with his favourite team of horses. His children would tell how he had trained the horses so well they stood over his body all afternoon until he was discovered lying dead behind the plow, his hands still on the traces.

The Dutch side of my family and their exodus to Canada was something I only thought about after the wildfire. They had boarded the ship *Tabinda* with one suitcase each, calling themselves lucky because they survived the War with everyone in the family alive. If they could cross the ocean and build new lives from scratch, I could survive a house fire with an insurance policy and a little help from the Canadian Red Cross.

Because, obviously, I was not going to have the same problems my grandmother did with the Red Cross. I was the first member of our family to go to university; I was the possessor of a graduate degree. I was an experienced bureaucrat who had worked in non-profits and government, managed multi-million-dollar budgets and large staff complements. I had training in conflict management, in achieving outcomes, in teamwork. I wore Hilary Clinton-esque pantsuits. I would have no trouble with earnest Red Cross volunteers who wanted to help.

My grandmother Vanstrien had a grade-school education, a fractured grasp of the English language, and a sullen streak. She could not have cared less about her personal appearance. Her grey hair was an unholy mess, including the ones sprouting from her chin. She wore shapeless dresses and old pinafores and stomped around in rubber boots, which she wore in the garden and everywhere except church. She never stopped working: even as an elderly woman she gardened like a farmer, growing huge plots of the lushest strawberries, the tartest raspberries, the firmest snap peas. She sneered at the efforts of lesser gardeners. Her gardens were explosions of colour, every space filled, with potatoes, rhubarb and *maggi* plants, which I did not learn had a Canadian name, lovage, until I was in my twenties. She had the best-looking pigsty on Wolfe Island, surrounded by marigolds and sunflowers and hollyhocks. She was also a drama queen, said to have once tried to leap off the side of the old *Wolfe Islander* ferry when she found out one of her sons was marrying a Protestant. (Happily married, they've been together more than fifty years.)

Whenever I hear athletes talk about "mental toughness" I think of that crazy old Dutch lady in the bag dress. She achieved her goal of being quintessentially Canadian in the manner of George Chuvalo, the Ontario boxer, five-time national heavyweight champion, and the inspiration for Hollywood's Rocky movies. She never, ever, took a step back.

I should have realized that if she couldn't crack the Red Cross, there was no way I would. I don't want to seem a whiner and I am

aware of the many blessings in my life. But of all of my experiences since the wildfire, dealing with the Canadian Red Cross is the one that left me feeling the most helpless, the most like a victim.

After the fire I took notes in a journal bought specifically for the purpose of tracking calls to services and businesses. Most of them take up less than two pages, cancelling the alarm service and cable, rerouting bills. There were more pages required for cancelling the gas and electricity, detailed notes about the hoops I jumped through— inexcusable bureaucracy given the energy company was operated by a regional monopoly. My grandmother turned out to be right about electric companies after all.

I signed up with the Red Cross the very first day that online registration was available. All evacuees were urged to do so as the Red Cross was designated as the main tracking agency used by all levels of government. Steve and I decided, with all the personal supports we had, not to go in person to the offices and add to the lineups, which was what the Red Cross was asking people like us to do. We knew desperate families seeking immediate help were lined up around the block at Red Cross offices in cities such as Edmonton and Lac La Biche.

We continued to wait while we heard many of our friends, none of whom had lost their homes, received aid via email and direct deposit. Other than receiving a registration number, we heard nothing. Almost two months after the fire, I started to call. Two months after that, I was still calling. By the fall I was walking the ever-changing volunteers through the process.

"You know," I said to the sixteenth person I had spoken to, according to my notes. "The cable company was able to help me immediately."

Even now, when I look back on pages of notes about the Red Cross, my stomach muscles tighten. It was the same thing every time: they tell me they are cutting back support because people are back in their homes in McMurray. I tell them I can't go home. A few minutes on, no doubt repeating a prepared script, they tell me they are cutting back support because people are back in their homes in McMurray.

I remind them I can't go home. They tell me it is first-come, first-served, not based on need. They promise to call within forty-eight hours. They do not call.

I had this conversation more than twenty times.

I thought of my grandmother and her grudges often during those months of repeated phone calls. I wondered, too, what it was that made me stop that day of the fire and reach out to snatch a framed needlepoint that hung on the wall over a china cupboard. I tucked it under my arm and put it in the back of the car, careful to lean it upright and to brace it so the glass would not break.

My grandmother, whom I never saw completely at rest, produced dozens of needlepoints over the years, samplers and pillows and random bits of embroidery. Many people who do needlepoint today buy a kit with a piece of cloth with a pre-drawn image traced on it and tidy bundles of yarn with the colours pre-chosen, a paint-by-number-style approach.

My grandmother was not a colour-inside-other-people's-lines sort of person and when it came to needlepoint she was strictly freehand. She sketched her own designs on pieces of rough cloth (too cheap to buy a pattern, my Aunt Annie said) and used scraps of leftover embroidery thread and yarn. She drew images from her mind's eye: flowers and animals and landscapes. As a child, I loved a two-by-one-foot depiction of a town with a giant duck in a pond. There was also a church, a windmill, a bridge, a sailboat, buildings of various shapes and sizes, a farmhouse and telegraph poles down along a laneway. The sky was the light blue shade of which the Dutch are fond, with brown earth, tall orderly trees with a leafy green canopy and bright tulips made of tiny scraps of coloured yarn.

An artist friend once visited our home and we showed him a new painting we had bought, something massive, modern and dark.

"Meh," he said. "It's okay."

Then he pointed to my grandmother's needlepoint. "What an amazing eye," he said. "The town is ready to come to life."

"I always liked the duck," I said.

He was right, though. There was something about it.

I didn't realize it was a real town until years after my grandmother's death, when I had arranged to meet my mother and her sister Joanna on a family trip to the Netherlands. They gave me a tour of Breda and, as we walked around the town, I recognized the bridge and the windmill and the church. We walked down the laneway with the telegraph poles, which led to the farm where they lived during the War. My grandmother had captured it in her needlepoint; it was Breda to the life. She went over its streets and buildings, crossing its bridges in her mind, bringing it to life in her busy art then hanging it on a wall and never telling anyone what it was. She never, as far as I know, created a needlepoint of Wolfe Island. But the town where she was born, married, bore her children, she preserved and visited alone.

I had been to Breda and stood on the lane with the telegraph wires, but I didn't understand what she saw in her mind's eye until after the fire. When I sat alone, I moved through the rooms of my home as it had stood when I locked the door and ran down the steps. I walked through the kitchen, stopping to straighten the frame of the Siapo turtle, a piece of Samoan art my sister-in-law Mandy had given me before finding out that I had always loved turtles. We hung it where I could see it while eating my breakfast, but there was so much activity in our kitchen, lunches packed and salads tossed, we kept knocking it askew.

In the living room I picked up one of the hundreds of compact discs Steve and I collected over nearly three decades. I heard the click as the plastic case opened and the whoosh of the CD tray sliding open on the stereo, then the sound coming through the speakers Steve bought for my birthday. I looked at the cover and remembered where we bought the CD, back before you could download music. I often played a selection in alphabetical order as over and over I worked my way through our collection. Yo-Yo Ma, then Dean Martin, then The Monkees. Les Paul, then Louis Prima, then John Prine. Doc Watson, then Duke Wellington, then Hank Williams. That was why I had always stayed

with the CDs, never putting my music collection onto computer. I liked being reminded of how we looked for a music store when we travelled, the hours we spent flipping through bins in record stores, and how we played music in the car on the drive home.

I can picture every detail of the home we made. The cool, smooth feel of the Inuit polar bear sculpture that had sat on my father-in-law's coffee table. The glitter that sloughed off the huge cardboard poster my sisters made, gluing old photos and headlines and funny quotes to tell a jokey story at our wedding. The bookmark Steve gave me, the first little gift he picked up because it made him think of me, left behind in a half-finished library book on my nightstand. I wish I could draw or paint or embroider and show you what I see in my mind's eye.

10 | THE FLATTOP AND THE DOBRO

MY SISTER CATHY, the closest to me in age, called to see how Steve and I were doing. We had been emailing and texting but she needed to hear my voice. As children, Cathy and I were never apart and later she skipped a grade so we went through high school together. She needed to hear how I sounded and I could tell she was beyond worried. We talked about when I was alone in the car in the traffic leaving Abasand.

"I was worried Steve and I were going to get separated," I said. "The longest part seemed the drive to get to him."

"That would be the worst part," said Cathy, "being by yourself."

"It was," I said. "It was hard waiting and it was hard being alone."

"I knew as soon as you got to Steve you'd be fine," said Cathy. "Even if he had to carry you all the way to Edmonton."

"True," I said. "But there would be a lot of cursing along the way."

We laughed and Steve, listening beside me, laughed too.

Cathy told me how my two nieces had reacted to the news of our evacuation. One spent the night glued to social media, reading every post and crying every time a report came in, asking continually if Steve and I had checked in. The other shut herself off, staying in her

room and insisting on keeping a mental image of Steve and me safe and sound, refusing to engage in any speculation. They spent a sleepless night, worrying if we made it out of town, if we had enough gas, if our old car would make the trip down the long highway.

I told her, too, of treasures I dumped into the car as I left the house, our grandfather's sleigh bells and our grandmother's needlepoint.

"I saved dad's guitars," I said.

"You should have let them burn," Cathy said. "I would have thrown them into the flames."

She would, too, and she had a point. I often saw my father's guitars, as Steve sometimes said, as a symbol of my best memories of my father because he was at his best making music. Sometimes I saw them, as Cathy did, as a reminder of shed tears and lost hope. Like everything from our childhood, they were both.

My sisters and I grew up afraid of dying in a fire. There were two reasons we feared our home would burn down and us with it. Those reasons sum up what it was like to live with my father.

I am the oldest child, the first born, and that I was adored was apparent in the pages of a worn green photo album of black-and-white snapshots. Toddler me wears my father's thick, Windex-cleaned, horn-rimmed glasses. I play a toy guitar like his real one. I babble into the microphone of his reel-to-reel tape recorder. My father looks on delighted.

Gerald Joseph Greenwood was a small man, like all the men in his family who lived on Wolfe Island for generations. The Greenwoods were notable for their longevity, living healthy lives into their late nineties. They seldom topped five feet five inches, their lifelong weight was one hundred and fifty pounds, and their hair did not turn grey until very late in life. They were fastidious dressers; my father loved crisp white shirts and shined shoes. He did not like neckties and when he played music with his country and western trio he often wore a string tie with a turquoise clip like the musicians he admired. He had a beautiful voice and was always playing with words. He loved

to sing-talk phrases and make up rhymes about birds and ice cream. Like all the Greenwood men, he was careful with language, never cursing until later in his life, when things were bad. Even then, he was an unimaginative curser and profanity stumbled awkwardly from his tongue.

He had few possessions, but his guitars were never far from his reach. They were always ready to play, sitting nestled in handmade wooden stands cushioned by a strip of velvet cloth. My father always wanted a Gibson flattop but we could never afford it, although the El Degas guitar I saved from the fire had a lovely mellow tone and smooth action on the neck. A brown and gold model with a thin, finely-tapered neck and low frets, he played it mostly as rhythm guitar, slung over his shoulder with a gold and black strap. His Dobro, a deep burgundy model with peacocks cut into the silver bridge over the resonating disks, had cost nearly one hundred dollars more than a regular flattop and was his life's great extravagance. In photographs he played it flat, nestled against his belly and hanging from a strap, using a thumb-picking style that was not showy.

He bought both instruments at Tremblay's music store on the high street in Kingston. Even though my father adored the store and it was within walking distance of the ferry dock, we didn't go in often because we were not window shopping people. When my father picked out a guitar, rarely for himself and more often for other family members, he went to Tremblay's and played the instruments. He had a great ear, although he could not read a note of music, and after he heard a song once he could play it. In most of my photographs he was playing guitar, and he looked at home with an instrument in his hand.

Towards the middle of my photo album, when I was about eighteen months old, my sister Cathy showed up. We sat in a plush armchair and I held her on my lap. Another sixteen months and Cathy sat beside me and we made room for my sister Kim who, although she grew into a gorgeously slender adult, was a chubby baby who looked like she might flop over. She was wedged between us so there was no danger

of her slipping to the floor. Another fifteen months and I hold baby Annette on my lap because there was no more room in the chair.

The rest of the photos in the album were of all four sisters. We stand in a careful row from oldest to youngest, like four stair steps, wearing matching clothes that our mother sewed on an old white tabletop sewing machine. To save money, she bought one length of cloth on sale at the fabric store in Kingston and folded down the same Butterick pattern four times, making the same outfit over and over, each one size smaller. My youngest sister, Annette, was sometimes forced to wear the same style of dress four years in a row as it was handed down from sister to sister. We were poor, I now know, or at least what the federal government would classify as "below the poverty line." I didn't know it then because we grew up in a community where everyone was in the same boat—certainly all of the small-acre dairy farmers, who kept chickens for the eggs and ate beets and pickles and jam that they home-canned from their kitchen gardens. But our home was spotless, our clothes tidy, our hair cut, our car washed, our lawn mowed, and our heads held high.

My sisters have copies of some of the photographs and I will cobble together another album. But the photos of me as a baby are gone for good, my having received all of them when my stepfather purged the clutter from my mother's house. I regret losing those photos of my father because he gradually disappeared from later snapshots as he began losing his battle with chronic depression. He fought hard, and for most of his adult life saw a psychiatrist, but his mental illness proved to be virtually treatment resistant. Every therapy petered out, every pharmacological approach ended with his sleeping incessantly or pacing our small house like a caged dog. The only treatment that ever seemed to work was the electroshock therapy he tried just after my youngest sister was born.

Even now, decades later, no one knows why electroshock therapy helps some people with severe depression. In a nutshell, it can affect chemical aspects of brain function and that can reduce symptoms, but

for many it still has the aura of voodoo pseudoscience and the stink of desperation. Until writing this, I could count on my fingers the number of people I told about my father's shock treatment and half of them changed the subject as if I confessed he was convicted of a violent crime.

For a few years following the treatments, his disease was in remission and my sisters and I had an easy childhood. We were surrounded by grandparents, aunts, uncles and cousins. The Greenwoods were part of what Steve calls "the five families of the Wolfe Island mafia," descendants of French and Irish Catholic settlers inextricably linked by generations of inter-marriage. We had the type of unsupervised fun kids had in those days in small towns where everyone knew everyone: breakneck toboggan rides, skating in the middle of the lake and berry picking in the cemetery. We swam on the flat rock shoreline and watched for herons at the hunting camp where my father worked as a guide and my mother did the laundry.

We sang, too, on the small stage at the local parish hall for Christmas and Saint Patrick's Day, where my father's trio was the house band. He sang funny, cheerful songs and the audience joined in on the chorus. He yodelled cowboy-style, like the Canadian country music star Wilf Carter, when he and his small band played at people's house parties. It was a mostly "dry" town and there was no liquor served in public or in private homes; even wedding receptions were alcohol-free with the emphasis on home-cooked roasts brought to the hall wrapped in tinfoil and a second "cold supper" at midnight with devilled eggs and homemade pickles. It was a laid-back life, punctuated by a few standout events like the first time my sisters and I became afraid of dying in a fire.

It was a cold, clear fall night about two years after the arrival of Annette and not long after my father's electroshock treatments. My mother had taken the ferry to her cleaning job at a Kingston hospital and my father was watching us, which meant he was watching one of the two channels that came in through the "rabbit ears" antenna of our black-and-white television and dozing on the couch. Our house

was small, five three-by-three-metre rooms plus a bathroom with a chemical toilet that my mother dumped every morning, carrying a bucket to the outhouse. My sisters and I were asleep in the bedroom the four of us shared when my Uncle Jake, my mother's brother, burst into the house yelling at the top of his lungs.

Uncle Jake, short for Jacobus, was Dutch, born in Holland like my mother, and the fact that he had burst into our home was a shocker. My mother's family never came to our house and my father never went to his in-laws. It was a Wolfe Island version of the Montagues and the Capulets, if Romeo had been a chronic depressive alcoholic. Adding to the confusion, although Jake learned fluent English at school (or fluent as the rest of the Wolfe Islanders) in times of stress he had a thick Dutch accent. My father, waking from sleep, thought Jake was speaking Dutch and Jake thought he was speaking English.

I heard my mother speak Dutch all the time to her mother and I could follow in both. I slid down the ladder from the top bunk and ran to the living room in my bare feet and nightgown.

"He says the house next door is on fire," I told my father.

"WHAT?" said my father, sitting up on the couch. His black hair was mussed from the pillow and he had taken his glasses off and was squinting. He was further confused because the house next door was a summer cottage owned by people who lived in Ottawa and it was closed for the season. Jake said something too fast and too loud for my father.

"He says the cottage is on fire," I said. "It's burning down."

"FIRE!" said Uncle Jake.

The next thing I knew I was being carried under my father's arm and we were in the bedroom. Jake and my father tossed my sisters and I into slippers and robes, carried us out and placed the four of us into the back seat of Jake's car, which had wide bench seats. We sat crying in a row as we watched a wall of red and orange flames on the roof of the cottage less than twenty metres from our home, stealing towards the lilac bushes that separated the properties. We could feel the heat

and watched ashes rain down from the night sky and land on the windshield. Over our wailing, we heard the snapping and popping of wood and the crack of flames.

I don't remember my father going back into the house or he and Jake carrying out anything except the four of us. At some point my father found the family cat and put her in the car, too, because my sisters and I were frantic about her. Perhaps he did go back in to get his beloved flattop guitar and Dobro but I don't remember him giving them a second thought. I remember my father sitting in the car and looking back at us and soothing us with his beautiful voice. I doubt he had fire insurance; it wasn't the sort of thing our family did, but I remember him talking as if it were the most casual thing in the world to watch flames creep towards your home. You would never have known he had been recently hospitalized in a mental institution and undergone electroshock therapy.

There was some drama when the volunteer fire department pushed my father's car with its tank full of gas out of its dirt parking spot and away from the path of the flames. The summer cottage was completely lost but in the end our house was undamaged except for some scorched lilac bushes and blistered paint on the side facing the fire—shocking given the care my mother lavished on our home. It would have been a different story if my Uncle Jake had not been driving down our dirt road that night. We would have been asleep as the fire spread and our clapboard bungalow would have gone up quickly. In those days adults weren't as careful about what they said in front of children, so we all knew it was a narrow escape.

By the start of the next summer things were getting back to normal for my sisters and me. We no longer panicked when the fire siren, which could be heard all over the Island, screamed to call in the volunteer firefighters. That was a good thing, because it sounded for every grassfire and burning woodshed and false alarm. Then a second cottage across the street from us burned to the ground in the middle of the night. This time, the cottagers were asleep in their

second-storey bedroom and fled into the road in front of our house. Once again, we woke up in the middle of the night to flames and loud noises and falling ash, rushed out of the house and into the back seat of a car, holding the family cat and crying for hours. The second fire did it. The four of us were forever afraid of burning to death, bursting into panicky tears whenever we heard the fire siren. Wherever we were, we would frantically head home as fast as our chubby little legs could carry us.

It's obvious we should have had counselling, given the nightmares, the sudden tears, and other signs that would not be missed now. Those were different days. We didn't have money for counselling; we barely had enough for dinner—and even as children we knew to cover for my father's "sensitive" nature.

We knew seeing a therapist was a shameful thing. My father's visits to the psychiatrist were secret and we never mentioned the doctor's name in public because everyone knew he was a "head shrinker." We never mentioned the Ontario Hospital, known as the "OH," the psychiatric hospital which people called "the nuthouse" or "the loony bin." The fact that my father had a shrink and had been in the loony bin, that he couldn't "snap out of it," was shameful. My father felt that to his core and was always resolving to "suck it up" and be "normal."

It worked, for my father and for us, as well as could be expected. After a few years, the benefits of the electroshock therapy began to wear off and by then bad publicity and the severe side effects experienced from the mega-doses then being administered meant the same treatment was not an option. My father began to lose ground at a faster pace, spending more time in the loony bin, which was almost as bad as being a repeat offender at one of Kingston's many prisons.

He was still trying, though, and he tried to take his music with him. The El Degas I carried from McMurray was the second flattop guitar I remember my father owning. He had an earlier one, German-made— my grandmother would have hated it—a gorgeous golden Framus with

purple trim and a luscious tone. When he checked into the hospital he took it with him for comfort and, no doubt, courage.

My father was a devout Catholic but his true gospel was country music and his father-son-holy-ghost was Jimmy Rodgers, Hank Williams, and Merle Haggard, those working-class poets of ordinary life. My father wanted one woman's love, happy kids, home-cooked dinners, birthday cards and church bells on Sundays. He found no romance in what he would have called the wild side of life. The songs he played for himself were sad and lonely, about hoboes dying far from home, prisoners who wanted to be sung back home, being so lonesome you could cry.

In the psychiatric hospital, he played songs about going home. He played for the other patients and for us when we visited, the four of us dressed in matching frocks, our hair pulled into tidy pigtails. Sometimes we brought dinner and sometimes we would eat outside on a bench overlooking the lake, the shoreline of his Wolfe Island home in the distance. We were excited to go to the hospital because when visits started it meant he would be home soon. But we were afraid of the other patients, some of whom had vacant stares and weird breathing and odd shuffles, despair hovering over them like smoke. Our father seemed different but the difference was likely us because while we visited he was not alone.

I don't remember if anyone else visited. In those days, when an Islander was in the hospital for heart disease or appendicitis, visitors stayed until the last possible second before catching the boat home. I hope people visited because it would have meant a lot to him, but most people pretended not to know he was in the psychiatric hospital. There were never other visitors when we were there.

One night when my father's guitar was stored for the night, someone dropped something heavy on top of the case and cracked the guitar down the middle. I can still see that crack, a fissure about two centimetres wide stretching from the bridge to the bottom of the

sound box. It was a great blow because my father lovingly cared for his instruments, polishing them carefully before setting them back against the velvet band in their handmade stands, and because we didn't have money to replace it. We didn't know how to claim compensation and the hospital didn't offer any. My father played the cracked guitar at the hospital but the sound was terrible, thin and tinny. When he came home and the guitar went back in its stand, the crack was a constant reminder of the loony bin. At some point, my parents cobbled together the money to get a new guitar but by then it was too late. My father had cracked open, too.

There was no music in the later days of my father's illness. He lay on his bed in a dark, silent room for days and sometimes weeks. He stared at the ceiling, self-medicating with cases of warm beer in stubby brown bottles, smoking cigarette after cigarette, Export "A"s in a hunter green package with a white border. My sisters and I spoke in quiet voices, afraid to disturb him and bring him shambling stiff-legged and screaming from his room.

Sometimes he got up hungry in the middle of the night and staggered into the kitchen to fill a pan with bacon grease and set it on the stove to heat. He would sit down to light another cigarette, pass out, and we would wake to a house filled with smoke. Other nights he crept out of his room and sat in the dark in an upholstered chair, the same one my sisters and I had been photographed in. He would light a cigarette and fall asleep, the butt would fall from his fingers into the seat cushion and catch fire, and we would wake to a house filled with smoke.

One time the chair seat smouldered for some time, burning a hole as big as my youngest sister's head. We woke in the smoky house, my mother a whirlwind, sweeping us out of the house in a sad imitation of the night the cottage burned down and Jake and my father carried us outside. She got us out on the lawn, dragging out my crying father. Then she and I went back in and I helped her drag out the smoking chair, which we put on the back lawn where it would not be seen from

the road. We did not call the fire department—because if we called the whole Island would know.

We could not afford to throw away the chair, so the next day my mother scrubbed it from top to bottom and stuffed a towel into the hole in the seat and put a blanket over it. It always smelled faintly of smoke, a permanent reminder that every night we fell asleep, we could wake up to flames.

Sometimes these episodes would frighten my father so much that he checked himself back into the psychiatric hospital. Sometimes he was too drunk to realize what he had done and my mother packed us up and we left for a while. When my father straightened up, usually after another trip to the hospital and a new course of drugs, we went home. As the years went on, the length of time between the bouts of depression grew shorter and the length of time we stayed away longer. Then one time we left for good.

My father died before my last year of high school, not in a fire as I had expected, but finally drinking himself to death. I went to see him in the hospital the day he died, thinking it another false alarm. There had been episodes when, filled with morose self-pity, he played on our sympathy by predicting his impending demise.

I knew this time was different as I stepped off the elevator. The hospital chaplain was there with my father's sisters and their husbands and they were saying the rosary, which the family generally considered an "in-emergency-break-glass" prayer.

My father lay on his back in a single white bed in a bright room that smelled of urine and antiseptic. Brown rubber tubes ran into his body. His eyes were closed and his mouth open. His liver had shut down and jaundice gave his skin a sepia tinge. He was enormous, his belly distended under the sheets. I put my hand over his cold, swollen finger-tips stained even yellower from nicotine. There was no sound other than his laboured breathing, the beeping monitors, and my aunt repeating his name and telling him I was there. He did not have a single grey hair on his head.

This time, of course, my father's guitars had not made the trip to the hospital. They were on Wolfe Island in velvet-lined stands, in a room filled with empty stubby beer bottles and overflowing ashtrays, by a chair with cigarette holes burned into the seat cushion. On a shelf nearby were four unframed photographs, lined in a row like stair steps.

11 | THE WEDDING MIRROR

I CAME TO THINK of the early days of the evacuation as a "thought experiment," an exercise in imagining outcomes like the Schrödinger's cat problem taught in first-year university courses. The Nobel Prize winning scientist Erwin Schrödinger pictured a perfectly sealed environment: a box that held radioactive material, a Geiger counter, a vial of poison, a hammer and a cat. In an atomic version of the chain reaction board game Mouse Trap, Schrödinger imagined the radioactive material decaying, the Geiger counter detecting it and triggering the hammer, breaking the vial, ending the cat. Because it was scientifically impossible to tell when the radioactive material would decay, an observer had to open the box to know if the cat was alive. As Schrödinger put it, the cat was both alive and dead until it was observed.

As the wildfire continued to burn, all information out of McMurray focused on fighting the flames and public safety. There was no information about the path the fire took through town or estimates of property damage. It seemed to me that McMurray was the perfectly sealed environment, Steve and I the observers, and our house Schrödinger's

cat. Until the box was opened, our house was both standing and destroyed.

Steve and I pictured different outcomes. Steve knew the fire skirted our street on the first day of the fire and held out hope for our metaphorical cat. My long wait as I watched ash drift down and smoke curl around the car convinced me the cat had used up nine lives. I tried not to say that out loud as Steve spent sixteen hours a day in a hardbacked chair, his computer balanced on a narrow press-wood hotel desk, posting reams of information online while never hearing a word about our home.

One afternoon towards the end of our first week in the hotel, Steve called me over to the desk.

"I think I found something that might show our house," he said.

"News from the city?" I said. "Or a media report?"

"It's an amateur cell phone video of a drive through north Abasand," Steve said. "Someone got in past the barricades."

"Do they get as far as our place?" I asked. We lived on the last street so the videographer would have to drive the length of the subdivision to get to it.

"I don't know yet," Steve said. "It's the only video I've found of our neighbourhood."

"We have to look sometime," I said.

I didn't want to. I stood reluctantly, took a few steps, stopping a few feet from Steve's chair. I looked over his shoulder at his computer screen while he clicked play. The anonymous videographer drove past the entrance to our neighbourhood where we saw the Welcome to Riverview Heights sign, weather-battered and in need of a paint job, still standing.

"That has to be a good sign," Steve said. "No pun intended."

"Maybe I've been too pessimistic," I said.

"We might be lucky," Steve said. "Look, the mailbox made it, too."

There was the community mailbox just past the sign, and I felt my heart start to lift. I took a few steps closer to stand behind Steve

and put my hand on his shoulder as the driver passed the first dozen houses on the street.

"Uh-oh," said Steve, as the driver drove around a slight bend in the road. Every building on the east side of the main avenue was gone. All gone, the houses with fruit trees ready to blossom and hanging baskets newly displayed on fresh-swept verandas and tricycles on walkways, even the house I watched being watered down with garden hoses. Every home had collapsed into its own basement, the lips of cement foundations outlining charred craters in the middle of ash-covered lawns dotted with twisted debris. The cheerful, noisy colours of the neighbourhood were washed out by a black-and-grey palette of dirt. It looked like a moonscape.

The driver moved on steadily, the street clear of obstructions because vehicles usually parked along the street had left in the evacuation. The voice on the video grew sombre as the truck rolled on, the camera panning left and right. Here and there, clusters of homes still stood, brown-stained from smoke, siding crumpled and twisted from the heat, roof shingles twisted from water bombers dropping their fire-retardant payload. Every single one was damaged—but still standing.

"There's a chance our house made it," Steve said. "We're the last street, we're close to the park so there were fewer trees and less fuel for the fire."

"There's a chance," I agreed. I felt my heart lift again. Maybe our home was still there. I had shut the last window, maybe the smoke damage had been manageable. Even if the water bombers drenched our home, there would be mementoes we could save: The bronze menorah Steve's father prized, a ceramic mug from my oldest friend Tim, Delft pottery my mother bought in Holland. Smoke and water wouldn't damage those things. Maybe we got lucky, maybe we could still save Steve's father's watch, his family's grandfather clock, the watercolours from my published stories. We could get some important things repaired. It was all do-able.

"I can't watch," I said.

I turned from the computer screen and walked back to the bed, propping myself against the headboard with pillows behind me. I looked out the window but saw nothing because my eyes wouldn't focus. I fought the urge to tell Steve to push stop, to pull the blanket over my head, anything to keep from looking at the computer screen. Once I looked, once I saw, the possibilities were over.

"He's turning the corner onto our street," Steve said. "The houses across the street from us are standing. They have smoke damage but they look okay."

I crossed my fingers.

"He hasn't shown our side yet," said Steve, "but he's turning around so we might be able to see."

I shut my eyes.

"Oh, no," said Steve.

I didn't say anything.

"Oh, no," Steve said again.

I opened my eyes to see Steve stand and walk over to the bed. He fell to his knees beside me and took my hand. "Our side of the street is gone," he said. "Every single house is gone."

"I'm so sorry," I said.

"I really thought our home would be there," he said.

"I know," I said. "I hoped you were right."

Steve climbed onto the bed and we lay there, side by side, holding hands. We were exhausted, as if we had just swum from a sinking ship to a deserted island. We barely caught our breath before the gaping maw that was Steve's work dragged him back to the computer, the email program beeping as new orders came in. Ten minutes later he was typing furiously, posting evacuation information, helping desperate pet owners. A few minutes after that I started on the first of the hundreds of practical tasks you must do when your home burns down. It was time to "get 'er done," an expression so popular in McMurray it could have been the town slogan.

One of my first steps was to pull the insurance policy from my Go Bag and call our insurer. I don't know what I expected, but it wasn't going to the front of the line. The day after my phone call our first ALE cheque was waiting for us at the insurance company's Edmonton office. It was a few weeks before we realized that ALE meant Assisted Living Expenses, the coverage you receive while the declared state of the emergency is ongoing. In all my emergency management training, I never put myself in the role of the person needing help. I was to learn a lot over the next few months.

I spent the rest of the week cancelling services and making phone calls. Like thousands of other McMurray refugees, we were figuring out where to leave our car, booking airplane tickets, doing continual loads of laundry because we had few clothes, buying everything from socks to medication to deodorant.

A priority was figuring out what to do with the family items I had taken from the house. The guitars and their cases, the family Bible, the framed needlepoint, the quilt, everything was bulky or fragile or both. We had no idea how long we could impose on the generosity of friends in Alberta; everyone we knew was dealing with the impact of the fire. The best option was to send items to family in Ontario eager to help and, we thought at the time, not burdened by worries about the fire.

I called the moving company that shipped our belongings to McMurray four years before and told them we had a few articles to send to Ontario. Maybe, I asked, they could also find the inventory list from our move to Alberta to help with insurance because we had lost our home? No further explanations were required for Trevor, the moving company manager. In fifteen minutes, he ran to his warehouse, found the inventory, scanned and emailed it to me. Then he started on the estimate for shipping what I had saved, a sliver of what we had moved out. It was clear I was at the top of Trevor's to-do list.

That was our first hint that the country was holding its breath until everyone in McMurray was safe. We had been in our own perfectly sealed environment at the hotel, surrounded by other evacuees. Every

piece of news there had spread like, well, wildfire, chewed over in the elevator, the lobby, the exercise room, the breakfast bar. We had not been expecting the same pitched interest as we moved into the world.

The moving truck arrived on time and I met them in the parking lot. Steve took a quick break from his desk to bring out one of our most prized possessions, a handmade mirror that was a wedding gift from a family friend.

"Be extra careful with that," I said. "The last thing we need is seven years bad luck."

"Don't even joke about it," Steve said, carefully setting down the mirror and heading back to his computer.

Trevor's local movers sent a large, freshly-washed cube van and two workers. The driver, like a lot of Edmonton workers, had lived in McMurray for a time and could easily picture the escape route I described. I filled him in while his associate, a small, slender young woman in a bulky uniform, prepared the packing materials. We were going over the paperwork on the driver's clipboard when, over his shoulder, I saw the young woman step from the back of the truck. She was wearing the proper safety equipment, including heavy, thick-soled black boots, as she stepped onto the nonslip treads of the step above the bumper. As I watched, her foot thrust forward off the step and she plunged face forward in a swan dive, throwing out her hands to break her fall. She landed hard on the asphalt driveway, her breath rushing out with an "ooof."

"Look out," I yelled too late. The driver and I raced to where she lay on her back, clutching her wrist and trying to catch her breath.

"Are you all right?" I asked as we knelt beside her.

She nodded her head and, through gritted teeth, said she was fine. Holding her wrist, she tried to sit up but fell back against the pavement.

"It looked like you didn't hit your head," I said. "But are you sure? It was a big fall."

She said no, she had not hit her head, and managed to sit up. The driver helped her stand and we walked the few feet to the back of the truck, where she leaned against the open door and continued to grip her wrist.

"I'll be okay in a minute," she said.

"Are you sure?" I said.

Her wrist was swelling and I stood beside her as the driver called back to their office on his cell phone and reported the accident.

"Will you be all right here if I go in and get you some ice?" I said.

"I'm okay," she said again, but she barely got the words out. The driver hung up his cell and I dashed into the hotel and up to our room where I dumped out a plastic bag of newly purchased toiletries and ran to the ice machine. I filled the bag and took the stairs back down instead of waiting for the elevator, making sure to tread carefully. The last thing we needed was another accident.

Out in the hot parking lot, I gently put the bag of ice on the girl's wrist and she burst into tears.

"I'm sorry," I said. "Did I hurt you?"

"You're being so nice," she sobbed, "and your house burned down. I should be helping you. It's just not fair."

"It was just stuff," I said. I meant it, at least at the time. "Let's get you sorted."

"It's so not fair," she said again. "I feel so terrible adding to your problems."

I'm surprised I didn't burst into tears along with her. It was so touching that, in so much pain, she was worried about our loss. I was focused, though, on getting her to the emergency room. "Let's get that looked at and make sure you're all right," I said.

One of her family members was nearby and came to take her to the hospital, where tests would show a hairline fracture of her wrist. After she left, the driver finished the packing in about ten minutes. Even with the layers of extra bubble wrap he put around our mirror, the items barely filled two boxes.

"Are you sure there isn't more?" the driver asked.

"I'm sure," I said.

"Do you mind if I double-check your vehicle?" he said. "There's been a lot of excitement and I don't want to miss anything."

"There has been a lot of excitement," I agreed and handed him the keys. He gave the car a thorough going over, examining the trunk and looking under the seats. There was nothing left to find. He looked solemn as he handed me back the keys and had trouble looking me in the eyes.

"I'm sorry," he said.

"It's okay," I said. "We're just happy everyone got out of McMurray alive.

"It is unbelievable no one was killed," said the driver.

"It's amazing," I said, "to go all that way without an accident, only to have one in the parking lot of the hotel. Life is strange."

"You can say that again," said the driver. He shook my hand, hopped into his truck and drove off with the two boxes that held everything we owned, our last remaining wedding gift stored in a carton marked "FRAGILE, MIRROR."

When people talk to me about what they would save from a fire, they often mention souvenirs from their wedding day. Long white dresses. Diamond engagement rings. Pressed flowers from a bouquet. Elaborately-framed photographs.

Steve and I did not pose for wedding photographs despite the fact we count some fine professional photographers as friends. We had candid photographs from the day that we treasured for images of family and friends, some now passed on. Steve's soft-spoken grand-mother glowing in a soft pink shawl. My spirited Aunt Jo and affable Uncle Bill doing the polka while the band played Johnny Cash. My good-natured cousin Pete—a butcher who elevated barbecuing to an art before the advent of television cooking channels—manning the grill at our outdoor wedding supper, searing perfect steaks and charming

guests with jokes and prodigious quantities of rye and Coke. He sang an off-key "Light My Fire" as they lined up in front of him with their plates out. I miss those photographs.

The mirror I saved was handmade using pieces of stained glass from the building in which we were married, a decommissioned country church Steve's father had restored. Roy's church, as everyone called it, was built by Methodists in 1876. It was a serious brick building with a bell-less steeple and tall, plain windows with stained glass primly edging the frames. It had none of the grandeur of the Catholic church I attended as a child, where sumptuously designed stained glass windows told stories from the New Testament, the names of each window's long-dead donor permanently etched on the bottom pane.

Roy's church stood next door to his farm and he had worshipped there as a boy. It seemed natural he would preserve it, replacing the brick in the steeple, refinishing the century-old pine floors, and building a massive fireplace where the altar had been. The work was finished just in time for our wedding and Roy often told us it was his favourite celebration—he always called it THE wedding, as though there were no other. It was a wonderful, laughing day in a place filled with light, food, music and people we loved.

Allan Morley Hunter, who made our mirror, was one of those people. He was Roy's long-time neighbour and the two men grew close after Al's wife became ill. I never met Dorothy Hunter, whom Steve's family adored for her quick mind. She had suffered a stroke that left her in a coma; she spent years in long-term care. Al visited her faithfully until she passed away a few months before our wedding.

We thought Al's gift to us was his contribution to the wedding supper. Everyone was pitching in. Roy made our apple-flavoured wedding cake; my sister Cathy decorated it. My mother supplied potato salad, pickled beets, and homemade casseroles to go with the red and white wine Steve and I made—the wine no doubt causing Methodist ghosts to turn over in their graves. Al went into his cornfield early on the

morning of the wedding to pick dozens of ripe ears, tossing them into a huge burlap sack. He built a bonfire with fuel from his woodlot to boil a massive cauldron of water and, while the coals readied, he husked the corn with quick movements born of decades of practice.

"What a lovely day," Al said, husking three ears to every one I added to the pile.

"It is," I said.

"It's a fine thing to watch a family grow up," Al said. "It makes you feel good when everything turns out well."

"It's turning out to be a wonderful day," I said.

"You can't ask for more," Al said. "Well, except for this." He laughed and showed me a special scoop he made for removing the corn from the boiling cauldron. It had an extra-long handle and holes drilled in the ladle to let the water drain when he plucked out the ears.

Al was one of those people who could make or fix anything. It was a great joke among Steve's family that any gadget Roy bought—and Roy loved gadgets like bagel slicers and wine aerators and cheese boards— Al would turn over in his hands and say, "A person could make something like that."

If Al had been born to a wealthier family he would have been an engineer or scientist, but he was a Manitoba farm boy whose mother died when he was young. He helped his family make it through the Great Depression by keeping things running on the family farm, coaxing new life out of old machinery they could not afford to replace. In 1943, when he joined the Fourth Canadian Armoured Division and went to war in Europe, he was so skilled at on-the-fly repairs they made him a motorcycle dispatch rider. Al's stories about the War were full of carburetors, radiators, spark plugs, bits and pieces of wire and old pliers, all of which he carried in his dispatch bag. He talked of missed turns and mistaken directions and claimed to have arrived acciden- tally in Belgium ahead of the Canadian liberators after misreading a grease-smudged map. He never mentioned that dispatch riding meant

you rode alone on dangerous roads, delivering important messages with lives hanging the balance.

After such a full life, it wasn't surprising Al wrote a memoir. Knowing I had edited Roy's memoirs, Al asked me to read his and give an honest opinion, which I did. Things were never quite the same with us afterwards. He was upset because I saw his story framed by losing his mother and his wife and his resilience in the face of great loss. Al saw no tragedy. He viewed his story as one man's journey through a world of astonishing innovations, starting with a horse-drawn plow and propelled forward by remarkable, transformative engines. He had held gaskets, pistons, fuel pumps and spark plugs in his hands and seen the future.

We were both right. I regret I didn't see that while Al was alive. I never imagined I would tell my own story through objects, one of which was the beautiful mirror Al crafted with his clever hands.

Only someone with Al's vision would salvage pieces of broken stained glass from the floor of a derelict church. The window had been smashed years before Roy began his renovation, the shards smeared with dirt and animal droppings, but Al gathered them up and carefully preserved them in his workshop. With the same sagacity, he collected pieces of burned wood from the Hunter family farmhouse he had shared with his wife until a fire destroyed it. That was Al's great talent, looking at smashed, derelict objects and seeing how they could live on, whether he was riding a motorcycle across war-torn Europe with a canvas bag of parts and wires or turning broken glass and scorched wood into a work of art.

Al's mirror is beautiful. About two feet high, it mimics the arched pattern of the windows in Roy's church. Al worked the stained glass around the edges of the thick frame made from the remnants of burned wood, now burnished and smoothed into generous curves. He left a typed message on the back noting the origin of the pieces, as well as the date and place of our marriage, something we have read again and again over the years.

When we rebuild our home, we'll hang Al's mirror and think of how he set aside broken things that he knew would be needed some day. We will look at it from our harvest table, which will have room for cheese boards and bagel slicers and all sorts of gadgets. We will look around us and think, "A person could make something like that."

12 | THE QUILT

IT BECAME CLEAR THAT, despite working around the clock from
our hotel room, Steve would not be immediately recalled to McMurray.
Workers who could do their job from a remote location were not being
bussed or flown in because there was nowhere to stay. Living space
for the emergency workers on site was limited, the smoke and water
damage was enormous, the electricity and gas had been off for too long.
Thousands of apartments, condominiums, homes, had to be cleaned
before people could get back in, and that included almost every hotel
room. In most homes, refrigerators were filled with spoiled food so
noxious that families were warned not to open them before throwing
them away. Washers and dryers, some abandoned mid-load, were full
of mould. Grocery store freezers and display cases were spoiled by
rotting meat, soured dairy products and decayed vegetables. The land-
fills were going to be deluged with material, but at the moment there
was no way to haul away all the trash.

At the same time, supplies were not making it into town, and there
were no workers at gas stations, supermarkets, hardware stores,
restaurants and coffee shops. There was a food shortage, a gasoline

shortage, and even though the water treatment plant operated through the fire, water pressure could still be needed for firefighting. The hospital was still evacuated, the pharmacies unstaffed, abandoned cars lined the roads where they had run out of gas and tow trucks and operators were at a premium. One worker in the Emergency Operations Centre later told us it felt like they were back in Kabul during the Afghanistan War, an image reinforced by airlifted pallets of bottled water and toilet paper.

We didn't know it then but even the homes left standing in our Abasand neighbourhood would need another four months before they were liveable. There was water to be pumped out of basements flooded when sump pumps stopped working, electricity and gas to be restored, roofs to be shingled and siding replaced.

We knew we couldn't go back and we couldn't stay in the hotel forever. We started making plans for what I came to think of as Phase Two of our evacuation. We found somewhere to leave the car, bought suitcases to hold the clothes we had somehow acquired since the fire, and got plane tickets to Ontario.

We started to realize how tough those first two weeks had been for our families in Ontario, who were getting their information from media reports, especially when our phone calls and emails grew briefer as we got busier. We told people we were fine, but they couldn't look into our faces, read our body language, see any of those clues that told how we were really doing.

It was a particularly tough time for Steve's mother, Donna Logan Van Vliet, who was gripped by the television news and obsessively reading online reports about the wildfire. When we finally made our way to her home in Ontario, where we made base camp in her granny suite while we figured out next steps, we realized she was under a heavy strain. She flitted about like a frantic hummingbird, trying to make us soup, to do our laundry (which we tried to hide from her but which she always found), giving us clippings she scissored from the newspaper. It did not help when a national newspaper ran a page-one

photograph showing an ash-covered crater on the exact spot our house had stood. She was often in tears, full of questions we couldn't answer, asking about timelines, about apartments, about work arrangements, listing off items to see if I had saved them from the flames.

She looked like she had lost weight and wasn't sleeping. She looked in pain. While Donna was a great proponent, even a proselytizer, of therapeutic touch and other body, mind, spirit practices, it was clear she was beside herself. At one point, she became so anxious I sat down with her and went over our insurance policy clause by clause. She worried, too, about our friend Ashley, who volunteered to work in the Emergency Operations Centre in the still-smoke-filled city even though she suffered from asthma. Donna also seemed to be fussing even more than usual over Hudson, the rescue dog she had taken in the year before.

We had been glad when Donna and her husband decided to adopt Hudson. They had been reluctant to make the commitment to a new pet. Three years before the wildfire Donna was diagnosed with an inoperable aneurysm and she spent every day after that preparing for her death, getting her affairs in order with the dogged determination that marked everything she did. She labelled everything in her freezer, organized her filing cabinet, reviewed her will. She told us frequently about her thoughts and wishes. She prepared so thoroughly for the eventuality, which had not come, that we had begun to believe it might never arrive. Donna believed it could happen any time so she chose a pet she did not expect to survive long after her, worried about leaving behind a commitment that would become someone else's responsibility.

The most generous dog lover could not have called Hudson beautiful. He was a solid, squat ten-year-old chocolate lab mix with a skin condition, and he scratched and nibbled away at himself, leaving odd bare patches. He smelled, too, a malodourous musk that could take over a room. Steve and I called him Big Stinky Dog and I didn't

like sitting close to him. Donna adored him and developed an elaborate schedule for his care. She searched the Internet for skin potions and dog psychology tips. She concocted an anti-itch moisturizing spray she brushed into his coat every day, laughing when she accidentally sprayed him with Windex, a mistake that did not seem to bother Hudson in the slightest.

"Hudson is improving so much," she would say. I didn't see it. He was still Big Stinky Dog, the labour around his care seeming endless and pointless. Donna was determined to make him whole.

He returned her devotion, following her everywhere, lurking around corners, his eyes always searching for her, plunking down at her feet. He plodded his smelly one-hundred-plus pounds into the cramped 1970s-style kitchen which barely fit four chairs and a table, where, despite our protests about taking it easy, Donna insisted on cooking hot, organic, omega-three meals, no salt and butter. She didn't like to use the air conditioning and as it grew hotter in the kitchen, the dog grew stinkier.

Donna was devoted to putting Hudson right before she died. She had the same attitude to the rest of her family. She kept constant watch over us, sharing news articles and website links about ways to improve our lives. I, a non-drinker, non-smoker, moderate treadmill exerciser, once made the mistake of drinking the cherry cola I allow myself once a month in front of her. The result was two years of articles about sugar content, caffeine, and the phosphoric acid used in soda pop dissolving tooth enamel. Whenever I visited, she sorted through the recycling to see if I left a pop can. I tried to remind myself that it came from a place of concern, but after the fire I found myself craving the hit of junk food—something so common after the fire that "Evacuation Weight" became a McMurray catch phrase. When I ate or drank anything of which Donna disapproved—which was almost everything I craved—I hid the waste in the trunk of the car that Steve's sister had generously loaned us.

It was Hudson we noticed behaving oddly when we returned to Donna's house after a trip away for the May long weekend. We had been slowly slipping back into everyday life, visiting friends and family and assuring them we were fine. We spent a quiet holiday weekend in Toronto, visited other family, telling stories about the evacuation over and over. I lazed about, sleeping and watching movies, while Steve continued working non-stop.

We arrived back at Donna's to find the house empty and Hudson wandering from room to room. The house was in what, for Donna, was turmoil. Unmade beds, cupboard doors open, dirty dishes in the sink, a teacup on the living room floor. Hudson begged to be let outside, where he anxiously walked the perimeter of the house, clearly looking for something, not finding it, and barking to get back in.

We were concerned but not alarmed, thinking that Donna and her husband might have confused the time of our arrival, for we had been a bit vague. It would be like her to think of something she wanted to get for us and race out to get it before we arrived. We made ourselves at home, Steve turned on his computer and I made coffee. Two hours later, Donna's husband walked into the house with dark, wet stains on his blue denim shirt. Steve was in another room and so he came up to me and said, "She's gone."

"Gone?" I said. "Who's gone? Gone where?"

"Donna," he said. "She died."

While her husband was out in his horse barn doing some chores, Donna felt the end for which she had prepared and called the ambulance herself. Two neighbours who dropped by the house unexpectedly found her, one racing up to the barn to get her husband. The ambulance came and an hour later Donna died at the hospital in her husband's arms. Her last words were "It's so peaceful."

Now, while her husband went to call his own son and daughter, I went into the in-law suite, the Suite Life as Donna called it, and told Steve his mother had died.

I didn't cry at Donna's death. It was about Steve, not me. And there were a million things to do, and Steve and I stayed on at her house while they were done. The next week was a blur, with family and friends in and out until the service. It seemed to me that I made a hundred pots of tea. I cooked spaghetti. I wrote Donna's obituary for a national newspaper's "Lives Lived" column. I picked out a guest book and a special pen for the service. My sister Annette came and made pots of chili and set out food for after the service.

I told people, too, how the last thing I had taken from our house was the last gift Donna had given us. The year before the fire she decided to give everyone in the family a quilt. She put great care into choosing one to suit each family member. Steve and I received a brownish-green bedspread the colour of earth, and shipped it to McMurray. That was the quilt I had pulled from the top shelf of the closet when, about to pull away from our home for the last time, I noticed the open bedroom window and ran back into the house.

At some point I started feeding Hudson, who continued to wander around the house looking for Donna. She had left the list of his feeding instructions taped to a kitchen cabinet, two-thirds of a container of his special kibble, salmon oil, a digestive pill, some olive oil. There was allergy medication, which I realized he was spitting out, so I started grinding it to a powder. Steve's stepfather asked me to use a pair of pliers to crush the pills, Steve's sister, a nurse, asked me to crush it between two spoons. I did both.

At first, looking after Big Stinky Dog was a "get 'er done" activity, to keep me busy and because I was still that person looking to contribute. My heart was not with the dog and the dog knew it. If I threw his red ball in a desultory way, he would sigh, pick it up, and trot past me, up the steps of the porch and into the granny suite to drop it at Steve's feet. He liked, I learned, when you threw it higher.

Steve had to be back in McMurray by mid-June. He had worked long hours every day since the fire, even on the day of his mother's funeral, toiling away on his computer from hotel rooms and dining

room tables. Now the human resources department at the municipality ordered all employees back to town under threat of termination, whether or not your home was still standing.

We were ready. One of our first acts after learning our home was gone had been to reserve a fully furnished apartment in the downtown building where I had lived when I first moved to McMurray. Steve and I were proud of our forethought because apartments were quickly filling up and fully furnished units were especially hard to find after so many people lost everything. We were early out of the gate and did well. Then one night, Steve got an alert on his computer.

"Yikes," Steve said. "There's a fire in McMurray."

"I can't imagine what else could be burning," I said.

"It's the apartment building we are supposed to move into," he said.

"That's not possible," I said.

But it was possible. Like every building in town, the apartment complex had extensive smoke damage. Carpets and curtains needed to be cleaned, refrigerators and washing machines replaced, and dozens of other tasks needed to be done to clean the multi-storey building. Something had gone wrong during the cleanup and now the exhausted Fort McMurray fire crews were fighting another fire. Steve and I watched online in real time as the fire spread. Soon the building was fully engulfed and, for the second time in a month, Steve and I found ourselves homeless. The upside was that we hadn't moved in yet so we didn't lose the few possessions we had left.

The downside was Steve had a deadline to be back at work, we didn't have an apartment, and rentals were at a premium. Steve would have to pay for a hotel when available rooms were being rented at extravagant prices to emergency workers. The Red Cross was offering reimbursement for returnees forced to stay in a hotel but we were locked out of their system. If Steve couldn't find something his employer would put him in an oil sands work camp but they would not accommodate me. I had to stay behind.

I spent some time with Donna's husband, a robust ninety-one-year-old who found himself alone on his ten-acre hobby farm with two horses and Hudson. I stayed off and on in the granny suite while I phoned and emailed the contractor, the insurance company, and people who helped us gather our possessions over the years, booksellers and art galleries, people who made furniture and sold cookware. I made lists of pots and pans, books, gala dresses, vintage tuxedoes, snow tires, tools, more books, and tried to connect with the Red Cross. In between my lists I walked the dog. I threw the red ball. I filled the water dish. I crushed allergy pills. The dog sighed.

Taking Hudson out for his last bathroom break of the day irked me. The lights on the little porch out back were on motion sensors and when the dog and I moved out of range they blinked out. Given that the old dog took his time, they blinked out a lot. Unwilling to step in dog mess or to fall in the dark on the steep ridge that rose behind the house, I looked into getting a simple on/off light switch. I found out Donna had always fretted about people forgetting to turn them off and thus wasting electricity, so Donna's husband gave me a lesson in how to do a shuffling cha-cha-cha back and forth to keep them on while the dog did his business.

When Donna's husband left for a two-week road trip to Calgary with his daughter, I stayed behind with Hudson. I could make my lists there as well as anywhere, and others in the family had returned to their regular jobs and routines and lives. I turned up the night before his trip without the carton of milk I promised and so headed back out to get it, and his daughter got in the car with me.

"You know," she said as we drove along the country road to the little plaza where milk was sold, "if you had to put Hudson down while we were away, it would not be the worst thing in the world."

I was taken aback. "He's not in any pain and he's got a good bit of pep left in him," I said. "I don't think it's time for any big changes."

At the time, I thought I was talking about big changes for her father but of course I meant me. I was getting used to Big Stinky Dog. Not fond of him, obviously. Used to him.

"It's going to have to have to happen eventually," she said.

Not on my watch, I thought.

Alone together for the next two weeks, Hudson and I fell into a routine. Awake at 6:00 AM for a walk outside, afterwards I sat at the computer for a bit with Hudson sprawled by my chair. Breakfast, kibble, salmon, pills, for Hudson; bagel and iced coffee for me. Red ball. Duck retriever fetch toy tossed until I tangled it up in the tree, too high for me to get down, making Hudson sigh. A daily walk to the mail box, slow and steady, watching the horses in the pasture switch their tails as we ambled by.

At 11:00 PM most nights I walked the dog up the hill behind the house, charging down when the sensor blinked off, doing a cha-cha-cha, charging back up to the dog, scooping dog poop with an old shovel, charging back down again when the sensor blinked out again. The dog sighed and plodded along beside me.

On most nights the belly-heavy Hercules aircraft, the workhorse of the nearby Canadian Forces air base, passed overhead on training missions as Hudson and I cha-cha-cha-ed up and down the hill, the farm being on the flight path. The planes were the same ones that had been on standby to evacuate us if the roads into McMurray had been cut off by the fire. Now they circled languidly overhead at altitudes so low I thought they might trigger the sensor lights. The dog was either deaf or used to it; the noise was thunderous.

The days went on. Reading. Insurance inventory. Trying to write the detective novel I had started before the fire, with Hudson at my feet, lying with his sturdy back leaning against me, lying under the ceiling fan, lying outside in the sun. Finally, I started seeing something in those brown eyes looking back at me. I started talking to him, asking questions as if he was answering me.

"Can you see the red planet?" I would ask between cha-cha-cha-ing up and down the hill. I downloaded an app on my phone to identify the constellations and planets, and every night we looked for Mars and Venus.

I finally figured out how to take cell phone videos and sent them to Steve. The dog curled in front of the TV as we watched the American Democratic National Convention. Hudson was running for office on a pro-red-ball, anti-squirrel platform. Hudson was listening to the "Chili Cha Cha." Hudson was listening to Warren Zevon sing "I Was in The House When The House Burned Down."

Then one night, we didn't do the cha-cha-cha. It was quiet, a bantam breeze blew down the ridge, and what the hell if the lights blinked out and I stepped in dog mess. The planes from the airbase weren't flying, there was no moon, and it was dark in the field behind the house. I didn't look at my phone for information about the stars, or hunt for Mars or Venus. I looked up. The sky was wide open, the Milky Way a brilliant, iridescent quilt.

"Well, look at that, Hudson," I said.

For some reason, I remembered a song that played on AM radio when I was a kid, not a country song, but a soul tune about things getting brighter. I sang it out loud to the dog. He sighed.

"I'm singing to the dog," I told my sister Annette the next day.

"Seriously?" Annette said. "Does he like it?"

"Seems to," I said. "He's stopped chewing at himself."

"Too funny," she said.

It was, but I kept singing until Donna's husband came back from his trip. He was surprised to find Hudson had stopped much of his chewing, his patchy hair starting to grow back out. I told him the crushed allergy pills were doing their job. I didn't mention the singing.

Four days after I left, off to spend a few days alone, Hudson made his last trip to the vet. It was inevitable; it had to happen sometime, a ninety-one-year-old man left with a big stinky dog who needed a printed menu for breakfast and spritzing with a specially made skin tonic. A dog who took twenty minutes to walk to the mailbox at a snail's pace and then had to take an hour-long nap afterwards. Anyone could see it coming.

"I didn't see it coming," I said to Steve on the phone. "I thought there would be more time."

"I did, too," said Steve.

"I'm surprised how sad I am," I said.

"You spent a lot of time with that dog," Steve said.

"I wasn't ready for it," I said.

"It's too much," said Steve.

"It is too much," I said. "It's breaking my heart."

"I know," said Steve.

Wrapped in Donna's quilt, I lay down and cried all day for that big, stinky, soulful dog.

13 | THE AWARD

I HAD IT BETTER THAN STEVE, who was forced to pay top dollar for a hotel and scramble to buy groceries and everyday stuff like a hairbrush and a dinner plate in a town where thousands of people had nothing and few stores and restaurants had reopened. He worked long days, went back to a room with no can opener, no spoons, no coffee mugs, to sleep a few hours and then do it all over again.

I opened our summer cottage on a deep lake north of Kingston and was alone for the first time in weeks. It was peaceful. Songbirds found their voices just before stunning sunrises. Mornings on the deck were perfect for drinking tea and doing crossword puzzles. The days seemed long.

I had been listless since we fled McMurray, something I partly attributed to having no books. An avid reader, I usually read two or three books a week. Now I went to bookstores and browsed the shelves, finding I couldn't finish the back-cover blurbs. I bought a detective novel and tried to read it for two days, scanning the same lines over and over before realizing I had read it months before. I renewed my

library card at the nearby small-town branch and my niece picked books from her collection for me. I read the same lines over and over.

I tried to write, partly at the urging of friends and partly because it seemed important to record events. I am a person who can write anywhere about nothing. I have filled cottage diaries with lengthy descriptions of watching hummingbirds and making Caesar salad. I once wrote five thousand words about birdying a pink golf ball on a tiny par three course in the middle of mosquito-infested woods. Now words wouldn't flow. I couldn't think of a single adverb. I wrote silly run-on sentences. I wrote point-form notes like "don't say all hell broke loose" and "too much hooptedoodle."

I struggled with my wildfire story; it was nothing special. Others had lost more or had more people depending on them. Others were alone and I was surrounded by family and friends. Others had no insurance and I had a good policy with a company that had an excellent emergency response team. I wrestled, too, with the life-time habit, born of my father's mental illness, of drawing a veil over family business. I would have liked to talk it over with my father-in-law Roy, a master storyteller. I found myself thinking about the story of which he had been most proud—and which had flashed into my mind as I prepared to walk out of my home for the last time.

A few months before the fire we shipped heirlooms from Roy's estate to Fort McMurray and our living room seemed complete, a mix of memories from Roy's farm and the years Steve and I spent together. There was an oversized leather sofa we bought because it reminded Steve of the actress Mercedes McCambridge's death scene in the movie *Giant,* his father's favourite film. Over the years scores of kids fell asleep on it watching Abbott and Costello monster movies on old DVDs we kept in the television stand. Sometimes the kids curled up in the massive armchairs Steve and I bought at a fancy furniture store in Kingston, the first time we bought anything customized, picking out the pattern, the legs, the trim. Above the chairs hung expensively

framed pictures, one of a Canadian flag over Kingston City Hall, the photo taken from the window by my desk at the daily newspaper where I worked as a reporter, the signed print a gift from the chief photographer. On the back of an armchair lay Roy's "Arnold Palmer" cotton blend sweater, which Steve wore on cold McMurray nights. The last time I was in our living room, I picked up the sweater and reached for the middle shelf of the antique pine sideboard we inherited from Roy. I took down of one his awards, the Gordon Sinclair Award for Excellence in Broadcast Journalism, hurriedly wrapped the sweater around it and set it by the door to take out to the car.

Roy loved that award, partly because he admired Gordon Sinclair, a veteran newsman with a stop-the-presses style. The two men appeared together many times on the current affairs quiz show *Front Page Challenge*, a staple on Canadian television in the 1960s and '70s. The award is beautiful and old-fashioned; there are no metal wings thrusting from a chrome base, no hard crystal edges. It is a smooth wood carving of a well-proportioned nude woman running, or maybe dancing on tiptoe, and it begs to be held. According to *The Canadian Encyclopedia* (we used to have a well-thumbed, two-volume hardcover boxed set until, well, you know) the statuette was nicknamed "Nellie" because it rhymed with "belly," which she displays in ample proportions. We had a photograph of Roy in a tuxedo accepting the award. We lost the tuxedo, which fit Steve perfectly, in the fire. We also lost the original picture but the chief archivist at Queen's University, where Roy's papers are in the permanent collection, later generously sent me a copy.

Roy received his Nellie—which he kept hidden away with other honours and family knickknacks atop a player piano in his stairwell hallway—for investigative journalism. It was 1986, towards the end of his lengthy career, at a time when his earnest style of public broadcasting and interest in spirituality were falling out of favour. Roy's lack of cynicism was often seen as a handicap rather than a virtue, and his

natural inclination for empathy and ambiguity, his on-the-other-hand approach, did not jive with the in-depth format of exposés. But with this story he scooped every news outlet in the country.

The story was about Susan Nelles, a young nurse wrongly accused of poisoning sick babies at a children's hospital. Nelles was exonerated after a federal Royal Commission and additional scientific research suggested the tests that indicated poison were flawed. No murders were committed but, for a time, Susan Nelles was the most reviled person in the country. Every media outlet in Canada wanted her story. I like to think she chose Roy to tell it because he saw it as the story of an ordinary person who, confronted with the horrific and inconceivable, took small, brave steps forward. Time and again, Roy returned to the same theme: Humanity's boundless capacity for resilience and redemption.

One day, I was thinking of Roy as I drove along a bucolic country road near his old home in Ontario's Bay of Quinte region. I rolled down the windows because the air conditioning wasn't working on my loaner car. It was the same type of morning that dawned the day of the fire: hot, sunny and dry. I left myself lots of time to get to my destination, which was lucky because I had to slow down. The road was dotted with snapping turtles trying to crawl across the busy thoroughfare and return to the bay after laying their eggs in roadside ditches. It's a familiar sight during the summer in Ontario, where turtle crossing signs dot highways. The signs were not doing much good. The twisty, traffic-filled road was dotted with sad, bloody, smashed shells. Carrion birds landed on the hot pavement to peck for dead flesh, taking momentary flight as vehicles drove past, then swooping back to continue their meal.

I slowed to a crawl and dodged every round object, even those small enough to be a stray stone. I tried to keep an eye out for oncoming traffic and vehicles coming from behind me. I thought about pulling over and carrying some of the besieged turtles across the road but decided against it. The road was busy and my attention span was not

good. I had been making silly, inattentive mistakes, leaving my bank card in the automatic teller machine on three separate occasions, going to the wrong coffee shop to meet a friend waiting elsewhere, losing my keys for a week only to find they had been in my purse all along. I didn't want to be run over holding a turtle on a country road. Besides, frightened turtles were known to loose their bowels on Good Samaritans and I had a meeting to get to.

I was also tearing up thinking of the turtle image on the Pacific Island tapa art my sister-in-law Mandy brought back from her travels. I loved the fat turtle drawn on the bark-cloth. Brown and black and circular, it was a totem of endurance and continuity, hard-shelled and steady on earth, free and fast under water. I tried to shake it off, to concentrate on the road, and to arrive on time for my meeting.

I needn't have worried about arriving late for my appointment, which was with the Red Cross. The building was locked when I pulled in. I waited outside with a friendly volunteer whose wife had dropped him off. We stood chatting and waited for the key holder who had been detained, ironically from my point of view, by a grass fire that forced the rerouting of traffic. I told the volunteer my husband's name and he asked if I was related to Roy, so well known in the area that a water-front memorial garden was dedicated in his honour.

"Yes," I said. "He was my father-in-law."

"The last time I saw Roy Bonisteel," said the volunteer, "he was in the middle of the road carrying a snapping turtle back to the bay."

That night I phoned Steve.

"I feel like your dad sent me a message today," I said.

"Did a shaman tell you a joke again?" Steve said.

"Not this time," I said, "and that happened a long time ago."

"It happened three months ago," said Steve.

"Seems like a long time," I said.

"You don't think you're getting messages from beyond the grave," said Steve.

"I don't," I said. "But your dad seems so close by." I told Steve about the snapping turtles and we were quiet for a while.

"It makes a person think," said Steve.

That's what he said the last time Roy shouldered his way into my mind. It was at my old job, a few weeks before the fire, as I thanked a young First Nations man for drumming an honour song at a public event.

"That was intense," I told him. "The drumbeats were pulsing inside my chest."

"You are supposed to feel that," the drummer said.

"It felt like my bones were vibrating," I said.

"The vibrations are the spirits of your ancestors," he said. "They enter your being during the song."

"Why would they do that?" I said. I couldn't think which of my unimaginative Catholic ancestors would be drawn by a drum.

"Someone has something important to tell you," he said. "You need to listen."

"I really do," I said.

"You really should," he said.

But I didn't. We talked about how he taught himself to drum because his parents were survivors of residential school, the same haunted site near the church in Fort Chipewyan. Now he was teaching his children and he showed me photos of his family dancing at powwows in traditional costumes he sewed himself. That was when my boss came over to tell him that a southern Alberta First Nation, a traditional adversary of those in the McMurray area, had given her an honorary tribal name.

"Do you know how my people bestow Indian names?" said the drummer.

Uh-oh, I thought. He's going to tell Roy's favourite joke.

"A boy went to his father and asked how do children in our community get their names?" said the drummer. "His father said, when your sister was born I walked outside and saw an eagle soaring, so I named

her Soaring Eagle. When your brother was born, I saw a bear walking out of the forest, so I named him Standing Bear. Why do you ask, Two Dogs Fucking?"

Roy's laugh, a huge, shaking belly laugh that echoed on and on, vibrated through me. I know how that sounds. Unlikely. Delusional. Wishful thinking. But when I got home I burst into our living room and found Steve stretched out on our leather sofa, wearing the Arnold Palmer sweater and balancing a computer on his lap.

"You're not going to believe this," I said. "I think a First Nations drummer just gave me a message from your dad."

"You're right," he said. "I don't believe it."

I told him anyway.

"It seems unlikely," said Steve, "and almost delusional."

"But I wish it were true," I said. "It makes me feel good to think your dad has a message for me."

"Well," said Steve, "it makes a person think."

I didn't think about it, not until Steve said the same thing three months later when I told him about the snapping turtles.

"It does make a person think," I told him. I hung up the phone and walked outside onto the deck of the cottage to see one of the bald eagles that nest in the area. It soared overhead in languid loops, coasting on wind currents with a flick of its wingtips, as steady as the Hercules aircraft that had circled over me and the dog in the night.

"Very funny, Roy," I said.

I went back inside and picked up his award and the box of trinkets I had saved from the fire. I lined up the treasures I had salvaged on the dining table and sat down to think about how a person could make something out of them.

14 | AFTER

"DO YOU THINK IT'S ODD that the only things I saved from the fire were gifts from people who have passed away?" I asked my friend Lucy.

"I don't think that," she said.

"Is it creepy?" I said. "It seems creepy that I was focused on dead people."

"I don't think it's creepy," said Lucy.

I was pretty sure Lucy would say that. I was pretty sure that's why I asked her.

"It was completely subconscious," I said.

"Was it?" said Lucy.

"Well," I said, "I wasn't putting a lot of thought into it at the time."

We laughed. I had said more than I meant to because Lucy has a way of sitting very still as she listens. She was one of the first people to contact me after the fire. She had said something like, "I want to remind you I am here when you need me. I know that is not now; it's not time yet. But when you need me, I am here."

That is how it is with Lucy and with the religious order to which she belongs, the congregation of Roman Catholic Sisters with whom

I worked for several years. When you need them, they are at their "motherhouse," known colloquially in Kingston (which clings to colloquial names like a toddler to a favourite blanket) as Heathfield. That was its name when the site was a country retreat for Canada's first Prime Minister, Sir John A. Macdonald. Macdonald's grey marble fireplace graces one of the main meeting rooms, as polished and pristine as when Macdonald stretched out his long legs in front of it. Heathfield is one of Kington's most handsome properties, a three-acre, four-wing stone building on ten hectares of prime real estate in the heart of the city.

I love the bustle and the energy of McMurray, its raucous can-do, hell-bent-for-leather spirit. I love its youth and vitality, its wide-eyed optimism, and its penchant for big, audacious ideas. I love the giant baby strollers, the barking dogs, the dad rock bands with top-of-the-line Gibson guitars, the cross-country skiers who zip around well-groomed trails in minus twenty temperatures. I love the go-go-go, work-hard, play-hard ambiance that permeates everything from midget hockey teams with top-dollar uniforms to a public library stocked from the latest best-seller lists.

I also love the quiet contemplation of Heathfield and its low-key welcoming of everyone who enters the building. I love the tongue-in-cheek Thou Shalt Not Park sign by the front door and the hand-lettered notices in the elevator that politely ask you to refrain from pushing too hard on the buttons. The corridors are quiet with rubber-soled footsteps muffled on the terrazzo floors, the frequent sound of feminine laughter murmuring down the hallways. It is made for the long view, with a patient expectation that life's purpose will unfold and there is time to wonder at humble things, flowers, trees, a sunset.

I waited a while after the fire to take Lucy up on her offer of a chat. I was still in Ontario and Steve in Alberta. Our home was not going to be rebuilt any time soon. We knew by then that we would be lucky to have a shovel in the ground within a year given the staggering number of houses destroyed and the short building season in the north.

It was a hot, sunny day—once again like that beautiful May morning in McMurray. I skirted the chapel with the feminine pink-and-purple stained glass windows imported from Wales and the enormous Québec-built Casavant Frères pipe organ. I passed the heirloom seed sanctuary and the organic garden blooming with heritage tomatoes, varieties with names evoking old-fashioned farmers in straw hats, Brandywine, Golden Boy, Yellow Pear, Snow White. Rounding the garden I headed towards the large outdoor gazebo where some elderly Sisters were enjoying the day. White-haired, with walkers and wheelchairs, they sat with faces turned to the sun. They were, I knew, wearing most of their possessions on their backs, just as I was.

Ever since I found myself possession-less, I had been thinking about the Sisters and their vow of poverty. Since the fire many people talked to me of "downsizing," particularly friends entering that stage of life when grown children start their own families. But they were not talking about redefining their relationship to possessions, not in the way that the Sisters define it.

This is the thing about the Sisters, and I hope I do them justice describing it. They have a stunning property in Heathfield and they consider it sacred space of which they are stewards rather than owners. As caretakers, they try to hold it gently, like a bird in the palm of the hand, and are always ready to let go.

I had been thinking, too, about how their vow of poverty did not mean a life of destitution. I have seen them take joy in a delicious cookie, a good detective novel, or an exciting Winnipeg Blue Bombers football game. They share a well-stocked communal kitchen, dining room and library. Their individual rooms are comfortable but uncluttered except for a few articles of clothing, usually modest "civilian" clothes, a pair of slacks, a skirt, two or three sweaters. Perhaps a blazer for official duties. One or two pairs of shoes. No jewelry except for the ring symbolizing their commitment. After death, that ring returns to the communal pot to await the next person who needs it.

There was that word again. Need. Did I need the possessions I had lost in the fire? Why did I save some objects—the rolling pin and the plaster saint and things I clearly didn't need? Why hadn't I saved the espresso maker, which I missed every day? I was looking forward to talking to Lucy about it, hoping she would help all possessions become meaningless to me. She waited at the reception desk to give me a hug and then walked me to her office, a large open room with comfortable chairs and sparkling windows. The room was simply decorated with Lucy's own photographs, examinations of light because she sees light everywhere.

"I've been thinking a lot about the Sisters," I told her. "I know that material possessions aren't really your thing."

"It's not about the material aspects of possessions," said Lucy. "Is it?"

"It's just stuff," I said. I probably shrugged. I was doing a lot of shrugging then. I thought Lucy was going to say "but it's *your* stuff," which is what a lot of people said to me, thinking of their own stuff.

"It's not just stuff," said Lucy.

"I don't need a lot of stuff," I said again. It is, I suppose, like me to argue with a person who has renounced material positions about having no material possessions.

"What do you mean by that?" said Lucy.

"Well, material stuff isn't important," I said. "I have a lot of good things in my life, marriage, family, friends, a place to stay. I even have a good insurance policy. A lot of people are worse off than I am."

"That's not the point, is it?" said Lucy. "The point is that you experienced a loss. It's up to you to say how big it was."

What she meant, I think, is that loss is not a competition. It is entirely personal. When you lose something, like the painting an artist friend gave you on your wedding day, only you can look into the empty space and appraise the value of what is missing. But if I admitted that, I would have to deal with it.

It was then, sitting in a comfortable chair in a light-filled office, talking to a friend who listens deeply, that I realized I should probably deal with it. But where to start?

Maybe, Lucy suggested, a writer ought to write about it.

I confessed I was having trouble writing. I had bought a special notebook and got out my lucky pen but my free-flowing "vomit-forth" style—what Steve calls "a human sausage machine"—was failing me. I could not move beyond point-form notes about times and places and weather conditions. I was researching the history of the objects I had brought with me from the fire, making visits to libraries and archives, photocopying pages in old books. I stayed up late scanning online articles about the manufacture of brass sleigh bells, the type of plaster in religious statuary, the origin of rolling pins.

"I'm not telling you how to write," Lucy said, "but it sounds like you're making it hard for yourself. Why are you researching as if this happened to someone else?"

"I'm trying to keep my distance from the story like an objective reporter," I said.

"But it happened to you," she said. "Why don't you write about that?"

"I guess," I said, "I don't know where to start."

That was when Lucy suggested a dream journal. I tried not to scoff. I had always considered writing down one's dreams to be the ultimate exercise in self-indulgence. If someone mentioned a dream journal, I'd quote Samuel Johnson and say I only wrote for money. But I couldn't say that to Lucy, especially because over the years I have shared puzzling dreams, which she would clarify with gentle but probing questions.

"What colour were the flowers in the dog's ears?"

"Where did the panda bear get the popsicle sticks?"

"How big was the door behind the golden chalice?"

It seems obvious now that my dreams after the fire were my subconscious mind frantically grabbing for my attention, that it would be helpful to examine those images of running up and down stairs, packing and repacking, waiting in long lines. But Lucy had to nudge me along.

"Make it easy for yourself," she said. "Write about the dream as it unfolds from your own point of view. Describe sights and sounds and

smells as you experience them. Forget the special notebook. Just sit down at your computer and start to write like I have seen you do so many times."

I took her advice, as I always do, and on my next visit Lucy and I talked what was finally becoming clear to me; the objects I took from the fire were sensory links, memory prompts, the intangible made carnate. That was when I asked her if I had been making creepy choices, which made her laugh.

"I can tell you what I believe," she said. "It's true for me but it might not be true for you."

"I'd like to hear it," I said.

"It sounds like you took things from the chapters in your life that were already written," she said. "Think about how those objects bring your story to life."

She sent me off that day with a quote printed on a lavender card, a saying by Saint John Chrysostom, another saint with whom I was unacquainted. When I got home I looked him up to find he was an eloquent speaker and writer—Chrysostom means golden-mouthed. He wrote, "They whom we love and lose are no longer where they were before. They are now wherever we are."

I think about that a lot. I think about the small box I packed when the fire came for me, a box I carried down a dark highway and sent on ahead to meet me later. I think about how my life changed in an instant. I think about how it didn't change at all.

I'm still afraid of dying in a fire. That summer in Ontario the province experienced its worst drought in decades. Flower gardens shrivelled, wells ran dry, and the fire risk was at an all-time high. I clocked fire exits everywhere I went and kept my Go Bag packed. I shouted at people who set off fireworks in defiance of burn bans. I shook my fist and honked my horn at people who flicked cigarette butts out of car windows. I kept the car filled with gas in case I had to escape.

One day I passed a grass fire newly burst to life in a roadside field. Utility workers were fighting it with the extinguisher from their

truck's emergency kit but the flames were six feet high and spreading. I fought an urge to race away and managed to stay under the speed limit, looking about me like a nervous chicken as I put fifteen kilometres between me and the flames. That night I dreamed again of fire.

My greatest fear, a fear I couldn't name, not even to Steve, was that the fire would always be with me. I visited it nightly in exhausting, effort-filled dreams. I rushed up and down stairs, frantically pulling items from closets and cupboards, knocking neatly stacked items to the ground, unable to reach the top shelf. I raced back and forth to the car, carrying random items, abandoning others. I was stalled in a never-ending line of pickups, ATVs, boats, babies and dogs, creeping along the single road out of town. The air conditioning was broken, the heat rising. I choked on smoke as the dandelion fluff of ashes wafted down on my windshield.

I didn't want to be there. I wanted to be choppering over it, tracking it by satellite, phoning in from a secure location. I wanted to spring into action, dispense wisdom and cold compresses. I wanted to be strong.

If I wasn't that, what was I? A homeless victim who couldn't get six hundred dollars from a charity that seemed a vast automatic teller machine dispensing money to everyone who once passed through town? A person whom other people saw, not as a warrior with a brilliant wit, but a tired woman crying at random kindnesses? Someone whose diplomas and books and scribbled ideas were part of a soupy mixture of fire-retardant spray, twisted metal, and cremated ashes in the cracked cauldron of a concrete basement? This was not where I was supposed to be.

But there I was, surrounded by signposts left by stubborn survivors and joyful storytellers who had gone on ahead. They mapped the way forward, those fixers, singers, gardeners, saints, bakers and snapping turtles. I could travel on, edging towards deliverance in a clown car convoy of funny, resilient maniacs. Waiting patiently at a dead stop or propelled at top speed the wrong way in the oncoming lane. Praying the fuel would hold out, ready to sleep by the road if it didn't.

So we drive on, Steve cracking wise beside me, in our dependable car with a well-worn rolling pin, a wedding mirror, and a plaster saint. We watch the blue dot map our progress, receiving messages from across the decades and sending back replies. We're on the road. Send prayers. Send bees. We're going to be fine.

ACKNOWLEDGEMENTS

WHEN I STARTED OUT on the long road home, I thought it was about the destination. It took too many miles to figure out it was about the journey and the people along the way.

George Hood was the first person to urge me to write this book. He and Debbie Hood welcomed me, offered food, encouragement, allergy medicine and the use of a printer.

George Fetherling convinced me I could write a memoir. He took long phone calls and agreed it would be hard work. He's a good friend.

Ann Lukits was the first reader of a manuscript that wandered into the woods, got lost and was almost eaten by a bear. She saved the day.

Peter Midgley believed in this book and championed it through the publishing process. Thank you to Kimmy Beach for her gifted editing, and to Cathie Crooks and the rest of the team at the University of Alberta Press for making it possible to tell this story and for your commitment to Alberta writers.

Thanks to Laura and Ross Cobb for the voodoo that you do. Thanks to Ashley Osachoff, Lisa MacLaren, Sheila Norris, Kathy Arney, Cynthia Beach, Monica Booth, Matthew Harrison, Alan McIntosh, Maggie Farrington, Frank Creasey, Kevin Thornton, Alan Roberts, Laura Lynes, Maureen Lollar, Tim Jaques, Axel Howerton, Robert Bose, and Glen and Rene Laubenstein.

Charles Linder at Unifund Insurance Canada deserves a medal. So do Shawn Chaulk, Marc Taplin, Scott Chaulk and Jaime Perkins at Stratford Homes, and Doug Caldwell and Brenda Carew at Caldwell Moore.

A special thank you to Lucy Bethel, Anne Hudec, Gayle Desarmia and the Sisters of Providence of St. Vincent de Paul for being companions on the journey.

Thanks to Rocky Van Vliet, Mandy Bonisteel, Jessie Bonisteel, Drew Bonisteel and Jay Primeau for being generous, honest, and caring.

Thanks to my mother, Nellie Vanstrien Greenwood Key, who did the heavy lifting for our family. Thanks to Kyle Bolton, Branden Coulter, Megan Cross, Nick Coulter and Emily Raite for being kind, clever and true; I am proud to be your aunt. Thanks to my sisters Cathy Cross, Kim Coulter and Annette Greenwood, for being brave, funny, loyal and for always, always, being there.

Thanks to Steve Bonisteel for driving the car. I can't wait to see where we go next.

Other Titles from University of Alberta Press

THE CHINCHAGA FIRESTORM

When the Moon and Sun Turned Blue

CORDY TYMSTRA

How the biggest forest fire in North American history
affected and changed forest fire management.

LITTLE YELLOW HOUSE

Finding Community in a Changing Neighbourhood

CARISSA HALTON

A young mother's extended love note to a city's storied
and notorious neighbourhood.

TINY LIGHTS FOR TRAVELLERS

NAOMI K. LEWIS

Vulnerable and funny, this memoir explores Jewish
identity, family, the Holocaust, and belonging.

Wayfarer, a literary travel series

More information at uap.ualberta.ca